A TEACHER'S GUIDE TO

READING
Conferences

A TEACHER'S GUIDE TO

READING
Conferences

GRADES K–8

JENNIFER
SERRAVALLO

SERIES EDITOR
KATIE WOOD RAY

HEINEMANN · PORTSMOUTH, NH

Heinemann
361 Hanover Street
Portsmouth, NH 03801–3912
www.heinemann.com

Offices and agents throughout the world

> Heinemann's authors have devoted their entire careers to developing the unique content in their works, and their written expression is protected by copyright law. We respectfully ask that you do not adapt, reuse, or copy anything on third-party (whether for-profit or not-for-profit) lesson-sharing websites.
>
> **—Heinemann Publishers**

The author and publisher wish to thank those who have generously given permission to reprint borrowed material:

Cover image from *Reading Instruction That Works: The Case for Balanced Teaching,* Fourth Edition, by Michael Pressley and Richard L. Allington. Copyright © 2015 by The Guilford Press, a Division of Guilford Publications, Inc. Reprinted with permission from the publisher, conveyed through Copyright Clearance Center, Inc.

Credits continue on page vi.

Cataloging-in-Publication data is on file at the Library of Congress.
ISBN: 978-0-325-09915-6

Editor: Katie Wood Ray
Production: Victoria Merecki
Cover and interior designs, typesetting: Vita Lane
Photography: Nicholas Christoff and Michelle Baker
Videography: Heinemann and Kevin Carlson, Seed Multimedia LLC
Manufacturing: Steve Bernier

Printed in the United States of America on acid-free paper
23 22 21 20 19 VP 1 2 3 4 5

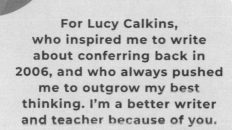

For Lucy Calkins,
who inspired me to write
about conferring back in
2006, and who always pushed
me to outgrow my best
thinking. I'm a better writer
and teacher because of you.

Book MAP

Planning and Managing Conferring Time 99

ABOUT THE ONLINE RESOURCES IN THIS BOOK

In the online resources connected to this book, you will find a variety of note-taking forms and other documents that will help you get started implementing—or refining—reading conferences right away in your classroom. For example, if you'd like extra support remembering the structure of different types of conferences, I've included handy table tents you can print out and keep with you to remind you of the steps of each one (see photo at top right).

If you want to be reminded of questions to ask and skill progressions to keep in mind within reading goals, you'll find separate note-taking forms for each goal that include this information and provide space to record notes about student strengths and next steps (pictured at bottom).

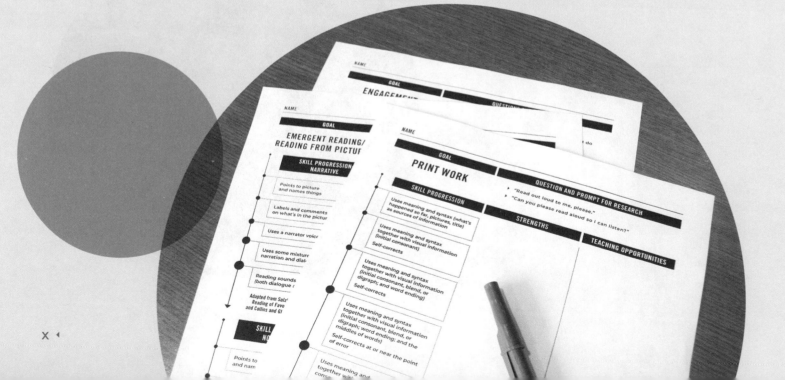

I selected each online resource to specifically support the conferring work you'll be reading about in this book. You'll see references to them across the chapters.

The online resources also include nine video clips showing each conference type in action with students in grades K–8. In the "Watch and Read" section of each chapter, you'll be invited to watch a conference and then consider the important teaching moves captured in the video example. You'll also find a complete annotated transcript online that you can use to study the language of each conference more closely and learn more about the thinking that informed my teaching moves. As a preview, here's a list of the nine conferences you'll find:

GRADE	STUDENT	CONFERENCE TYPE
1	Ian	Assessment
5	Gavin	Goal Setting
8	Justin	Compliment
2	Lucas	Research-Compliment-Teach
K	Ana	Coaching
K	Group of students	Strategy Lesson
8	Group of students	Strategy Lesson
K	Gabbie and Ashley	Partnership
4	Group of students	Book Club

To access the online resources, visit

http://hein.pub/ClassroomEssentials-login

Enter your email address and password (or click "Create New Account" to set up an account).

Once you have logged in, enter keycode

CEREADCON

and click "Register."

chapter one

GETTING YOUR CLASSROOM
Conferring-Ready

What Is Conferring? Why Confer?

When you confer, you tailor your instruction to each student's strengths and needs. But you do so much more than that.

Conferring is where the magic happens. It's the heartbeat of the literacy block.

Conferring helps teachers do the important work of seeing the rich and beautiful variety of individual students in the classroom, and to honor and cherish where each student is with their learning (Paley 2000). When you work one-on-one or in small groups with students, it allows you to value each child's language and literacy practices, and their own literacy development, and to treat each child as a competent learner (Ladson-Billings 2009; Souto-Manning and Martell 2016). Conferring blurs the lines between teacher and student; you become a researcher as you learn about your students, and they learn from you (Morrell 2012; Freire 1998).

Routman (2003) has written that one of the strongest predictors of reading achievement is the quality of the teacher-student relationship. In reading conferences, you give a student or group of students your undivided attention, and develop strong relationships with them.

There are a variety of types of individual and small-group conferences, each with a unique structure and purpose and consistent student and teacher roles.

During conferences:

▸ **Students** are expected to self-reflect, show what they've learned, ask for support, and practice strategies.

▸ **Teachers** offer new strategies or support for ones still being practiced, give feedback, and guide readers.

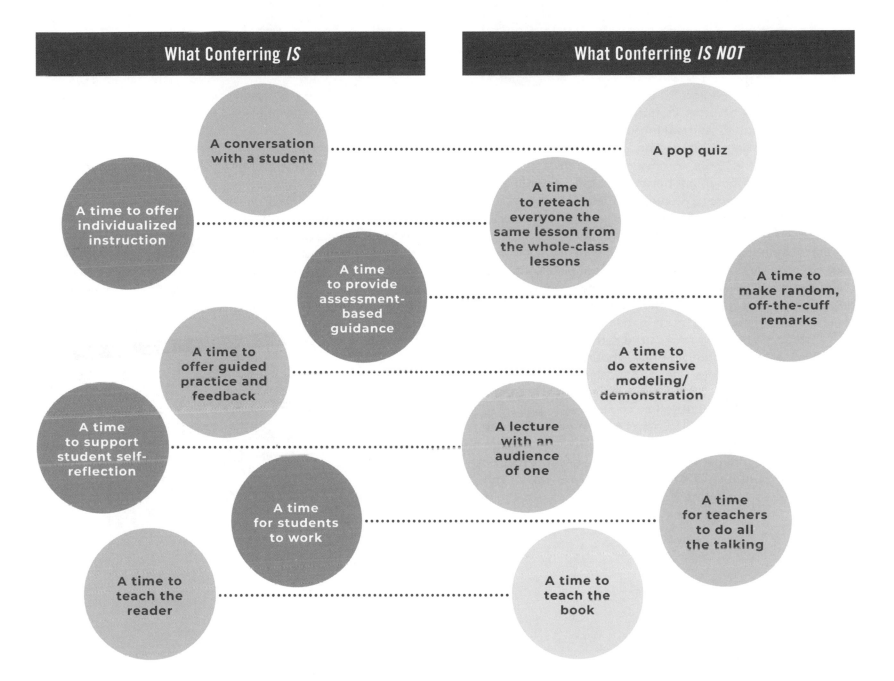

What Conferring *IS*

- A conversation with a student
- A time to offer individualized instruction
- A time to provide assessment-based guidance
- A time to offer guided practice and feedback
- A time to support student self-reflection
- A time for students to work
- A time to teach the reader

What Conferring *IS NOT*

- A pop quiz
- A time to reteach everyone the same lesson from the whole-class lessons
- A time to make random, off-the-cuff remarks
- A time to do extensive modeling/demonstration
- A lecture with an audience of one
- A time for teachers to do all the talking
- A time to teach the book

But . . . What Is the *Rest* of the Class Doing?

The short answer? Reading. Sure, you could keep the rest of the class busy with other literacy-related activities while you confer, but the most meaningful (and enjoyable!) thing students can be doing is engaging with texts of their own choosing. Since the 1980s, compelling research has shown that what helps children get better at reading is reading (Allington 2011; Anderson, Wilson, and Fielding 1988; Krashen 2004; Cunningham and Allington 1999; Miller 2009). Shocking, I know! Even as teachers have made time for independent reading, reading-related activities that are holdovers from the past—decodable readers, reading centers and stations, basal readers, comprehension question worksheets, phonics activities, memorizing sight words, and more—still take up too much time in the reading block in many classrooms.

Instead of spending time at the Xerox machine running off worksheets or spending countless hours creating materials for centers, get books in students' hands and *let them read.* Once students are set up with books, comfortable reading spots, and uninterrupted time, you can be free to pull small groups and/or to work with students one-on-one. And once you've started conferring and teaching students the strategies they need most, independent reading time becomes purposeful, highly accountable, and even more powerful (Miller and Moss 2013; Moss and Young 2010).

HOW MUCH TIME, HOW MANY BOOKS, HOW MANY KIDS A DAY?

I recommend you try to check in with each of your students and support their individual reading goals twice a week, *somehow.* It could be a small group and a conference, two small groups, or two conferences. For a class of twenty-five students, that means you'll try to meet with ten students a day (25 kids × 2 times a week = 50 kids a week ÷ 5 days in a week = 10 students a day).

With the ten-a-day aim in mind, it's important to build students' stamina and set them up to read and practice their strategies independently for a sustained block of time. You'll need to set aside enough minutes in your schedule and also have enough books available to keep children reading for the whole time.

 At the end of this book, you'll learn about how to plan your conferring time using a simple schedule. A blank of this form is available in the online resources.

Grade Level	Approximate Number of Minutes of In-Class Reading, Daily
Kindergarten	▸ 7–20 minutes: independent reading and conferring ▸ 5–10 minutes: partner reading and conferring
First	▸ 15–25 minutes: independent reading and conferring ▸ 5–10 minutes: partner reading and conferring
Second	▸ 20–35 minutes: independent reading and conferring ▸ 5–10 minutes: partner reading and conferring
Third through fifth	▸ 40–45 minutes: independent reading and conferring ▸ 10+ minutes: twice weekly, subtract some time from independent reading to allow for partnership or club time and conferring
Middle school	Bell schedules and reading periods vary. Take the number of minutes for the entire reading period and subtract 15–20 minutes for whole-class instruction. What's not being used for whole-class instruction can be used for independent reading with conferring.

My recommendations for the number of minutes children should be reading *in school each day*.

Notice there is a range of recommended times for each grade level. At the beginning of the year, before building stamina and routines, you may find you need to go with the lower end of the range. By the end of the first or second month of school, many children can read toward the upper end of the range. An important word of caution: Don't just set the clock and expect students to read for forty minutes; talk with kids about strategies for building up to that time while staying engaged (see Chapter 2 in *The Reading Strategies Book* [Serravallo 2015] for more ideas to support reading engagement).

As you look at the recommendations for independent reading minutes by grade level, notice that for the primary grades I'm recommending daily independent and partner reading. This helps extend children's stamina because the transition from independent to partner reading is a change in activity.

While children read independently, the teacher confers with individuals and small groups. While children work with partners and discuss books with peers, the teacher is also conferring.

Children are also ideally reading at home and on the weekends. All of this reading time means children will need access to many books. Based on word-per-minute–rate research (Harris and Sipay 1990) and the recommended number of minutes students should read each week, the chart at the right offers a suggested quantity of books children should choose each week from the school and/or classroom library. Depending on their out-of-school reading habits, they may need even more books than I recommend in the chart.

Throughout this book I have chosen to use the term *emergent bilingual* to refer to children who are in the continual process of learning language (García et al. 2008; Ascenzi-Moreno 2018). Speaking two or more languages is a strength which should be respected and valued in the classroom and is an important part of students' identities as learners. It is also an additional consideration for reading teachers, which is why special spotlights are included in every chapter of this book, with numerous citations to learn more. You'll see the first of these spotlights on the opposite page.

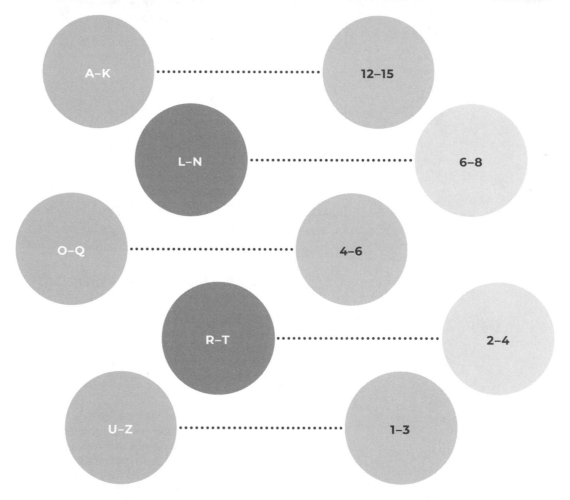

Book Level*	Approximate Number of Books Each Student Needs to Sustain Reading for the Week
A–K	12–15
L–N	6–8
O–Q	4–6
R–T	2–4
U–Z	1–3

*The letters refer to a leveling system used throughout this book, the F&P Text Level Gradient™. If you use another leveling system, you can find Fountas and Pinnell's correlation chart at www.fountasandpinnell.com/textlevelgradient/.

SETTING UP A CLASSROOM LIBRARY

Ideally, you will have a well-stocked, well-organized classroom library filled with an inclusive collection of fiction and nonfiction that helps students both see themselves in the books they read and learn about the world (Bishop 1990). A crucial component to student engagement is matching readers with high-quality texts by authors they want to read and about topics they are interested in exploring (Miller 2009; Miller and Moss 2013).

For students to find what they are looking for quickly, the library will need to be open and inviting, with labeled bins so children can easily match their own interests with books. While you may choose to mark each of the books with the text's level in a discreet place (such as the inside front cover), libraries organized by author, genre, topic, and themes will help students think about their own reading identities as the primary driver of their choices (Serravallo 2018). For more advice on filling and funding book rooms and classroom libraries, and organizing your collection, I recommend *It's All About the Books* (Mulligan and Landrigan 2018).

Spotlight on EMERGENT BILINGUALS

Tips for Book Selections

▸ Don't limit students' choices, as their cognitive abilities, background knowledge, and interests may far exceed what they are able to read with complete accuracy, fluency, and comprehension in English (Moses 2015).

▸ Because readers can match pictures with words, highly visual texts (picture books, wordless books, concept books, graphic novels) offer students added support, and (because they are universal) images also facilitate talk across languages.

▸ Consider also the power of text sets—multiple texts around a common topic where students will see the same or similar vocabulary used over and over.

▸ If students are able to read in their first languages, you might search for books written in those languages, as literacy development in one language supports development in another (Wallace 2013).

▸ Depending on the age of your students, a dual-language dictionary, perhaps one with pictures, can help students translate unfamiliar words as they read independently.

Preparing an Environment for Conferring

Perhaps you looked at the recommendations in the last section and thought "that's a lot of minutes" or "that's a lot of books." Yes, it is. But it is absolutely possible for students to accomplish that level of independence and engagement with careful instruction, clear expectations, engaging books, and a well-thought-out environment (Hertz and Mraz 2018). Additionally, classrooms that are inclusive, and reflect the diversities of the students in your room, will help all students feel comfortable and empowered (Earick 2009). Reflect on the following questions to see if there are ways you might modify the physical space or how it's used to offer more support for your readers:

▶ Do students choose where to sit for independent reading? If you can offer choice, students may be able to create their best reading conditions (dim/bright lighting; soft seat/hard chair; seated/lying down; quiet/noisy; and so on).

▶ Do students have access to materials they may need? Think about why students interrupt you for help and create a materials center that includes sticky notes, sharpened pencils, etc.

▶ Are there charts in the room that offer students reminders of strategies? Are they current and targeted to what students need? Can any clutter or visual "noise" be eliminated to simplify and quiet the environment?

▶ Are all students' identities reflected in the classroom and do they feel a part of the classroom community?

▶ Are there systems in place for children to transition quickly between whole-class lessons, independent reading, partner, or book club reading? Is the room open enough to allow those transitions to happen smoothly?

What Are the Types of Conferences I'll Read About in This Book?

In the chapters ahead, you'll read about the different types of confer-ences you see on the book map on pages vii–ix. The book is organized in the order you're most likely to use the conference types as you get started. Assessment conferences will help you get to know your readers, and then once you do, meeting with them in Goal-Setting Conferences helps you establish goals. As soon as everyone has goals, you can offer positive feed-back (Compliment Conferences) and support those goals with strategies (Coaching and Research-Compliment-Teach Conferences). Once you start noticing patterns in what your students need, it makes sense to work efficiently and pull small-group Strategy Lessons. Once that feels solid, you might shift your attention to conferring during the conversation and collaboration time (Partnership and Club Conferences). In the final chapter, I offer advice for how to use each type of conference with purpose and at a time that will be most helpful to you.

When to Use Each Type of Conference

Assessment (or other assessments)

Goal Setting

Teaching one-on-one (Compliment, Coaching, Research-Compliment-Teach)

Teaching in a group (Strategy Lesson)

Teaching partnerships or clubs during talk (Partnership/Club)

RICHARD ALLINGTON

Richard Allington is a must-know researcher in the field of reading instruction. His books are accessible, and the ideas within them are beautiful in their simplicity and power. If you have the chance to hear him speak at a conference or workshop, you'll likely find that he doesn't mince words: he speaks with passion and truth. He is one of the researchers I mention most in my own work, but I highly recommend you check out some of his work so you can hear it straight from the source.

FOURTH EDITION

READING INSTRUCTION THAT WORKS
The Case for Balanced Teaching

Michael Pressley
Richard L. Allington

{ My Top Must-Read Texts by Richard Allington }

What Really Matters for Struggling Readers: Designing Research-Based Programs, 3rd ed. Allington, Richard L. 2011.

I have been carrying this book into schools and quoting it frequently since the first edition was published in 2001. The research (updated across three editions) Allington reviews is compelling and his advice is practical: if we want kids to become better readers, we've got to let them read, we've got to provide them with books, and we've got to give them plenty of experience with fluent, successful reading.

Classrooms That Work: Where All Children Read and Write, 6th ed. Cunningham, Patricia, and Richard L. Allington. 2015.

I read the first edition when I was studying to be a teacher. Emphasizing authentic experiences with texts, this is a foundational text about balanced literacy. Special attention is paid to making sure instruction meets all students' needs, especially students from diverse backgrounds and those who may struggle with literacy.

What Really Matters in Response to Intervention: Research-Based Designs. Allington, Richard L. 2008.

This book reminds us how crucial it is to really tailor intervention plans to what students need and what research says works so we don't fall into the trap of purchasing costly programs that won't help readers. Spoiler alert: Lots of high-volume reading of just-right texts outweighs skill-and-drill practice for intervention students.

Conferring is where the magic happens. It's the heartbeat of the literacy block.

chapter two

Understanding
WHAT READERS KNOW AND NEED

The first step to make conferring feel more doable for you, and to maximize its usefulness for students, is to make sure it's purposeful. You're one-on-one with a student, so why waste time teaching something the student doesn't need or something that's way out of the scope of what they can practice? An Assessment Conference offers you a little time to study a reader along a number of different dimensions, considering a variety of possible goals. These conferences can set you both up to focus during future conferring time and can help students focus during the independent practice time.

All conferences offer some chance to assess. With eyes open, it's possible to get feedback every day from students about how they are working on strategies you've taught, how they are making gains toward their goals, what they struggle with, and what new learning they've taken on since you last met with them. An Assessment Conference is really a deeper dive into assessment where you explore all or most of the possible goals. You may end an Assessment Conference with a bit of feedback or even offer the reader a tip—but the majority of the time is spent assessing the student and encouraging student self-reflection.

In an Assessment Conference, I first consider all the possible goals I might have for any reader and then think about ways to assess each one. To the right is a "hierarchy of goals," originally published in *The Reading Strategies Book* (Serravallo 2015). This list of goals is how I categorize and organize my thinking about reading. While all goals on this list are equally important, it's arranged in an intentional order—with goals I'd address first at the top and goals I'd address later toward the bottom.

When I am working with a student in an Assessment Conference, I use a conversational tone and learn about the student through prompts and questions connected to each goal category. I may choose to look at student work samples, ask students to self-reflect, and/or provide students with an opportunity to demonstrate their skills. With each response from the child, I'm comparing what they offer to what I'd expect for a student reading books at the level of complexity they're reading.

Hierarchy of Reading Goals

Emergent Reading

Engagement

Print Work

Fluency

Comprehension

Fiction/Literature — Nonfiction/Information

Plot & Setting — Main Idea

Character — Key Details

Vocabulary & Figurative Language — Vocabulary

Themes & Ideas — Text Features

Conversation

Writing About Reading

From *The Reading Strategies Book* (Serravallo 2015)

*An Assessment Conference
offers you a little time
to study a reader along
a number of different
dimensions, considering
a variety of possible goals.*

Aligning Goals, Skills, Assessments, and Questions

In the table that follows, you'll find each goal from the hierarchy unpacked. In the second row is a list of the reading skills that I consider to be a part of each goal. In the third row you'll find a list of suggested assessments that you might already have or may want to incorporate that will help you determine if the goal is right for the student you're thinking about. You can find more information about any of these assessments in *The Reading Strategies Book* (Serravallo 2015) or The Literacy Teacher's Playbook series (Serravallo 2012, 2013). And in the final row you'll find a list of questions or prompts that you can use during an Assessment Conference—or really during any conference—to learn more about a student's work within each potential goal area. For a note-taking form to keep on a clipboard as you try this type of conference, see the online resources. 🖥

Goal-aligned assessments and prompts for assessing readers

Goal	READING FROM PICTURES	ENGAGEMENT	PRINT WORK
Skills	Using pictures to tell a story or tell information from a nonfiction text	▸ Focus ▸ Stamina ▸ Book choice	▸ Decoding ▸ Monitoring ▸ Self-correcting
Assessments	▸ Sulzby's (1985) Emergent Storybook Categories ▸ Collins and Glover's (2015) categories for assessing familiar and unfamiliar fiction and nonfiction reading	▸ Reading logs ▸ Engagement inventory ▸ Interest survey	▸ Running record
Questions or Prompts	▸ *[using a familiar book that's been read aloud to the student]* "Read to me." *[with the expectation that the reading is happening from the pictures]* ▸ *[fiction]* "Tell me this story, using the pictures." ▸ *[nonfiction]* "Tell me about what you're learning in this book."	▸ "What made you choose this book?" ▸ "When you go to the library to choose a book, what do you think about?" ▸ "When do you choose to read?" ▸ "Do you read even if it's not assigned?" ▸ "When you read, do you find that you get distracted?" ▸ *[if the student answers yes to the question above]* "What do you do to refocus?"	▸ "Read out loud to me, please."

Goal	FLUENCY	COMPREHENSION: PLOT AND SETTING	COMPREHENSION: CHARACTER	COMPREHENSION: VOCABULARY AND FIGURATIVE LANGUAGE
Skills	▸ Phrasing ▸ Reading with intonation and expression ▸ Automaticity	▸ Retelling ▸ Synthesizing cause and effect ▸ Synthesizing problem and solution ▸ Visualizing setting	▸ Inferring and interpreting main and secondary characters ▸ Synthesizing character change ▸ Inferring and interpreting character relationships	▸ Monitoring for meaning and inferring to determine the meaning of words and phrases
Assessments	▸ Running record ▸ Fluency record	▸ Whole-book assessment ▸ Conferring ▸ Retell portion of running record	▸ Whole-book assessment ▸ Conferring ▸ Selected questions from running records	▸ Whole-book assessment ▸ Conferring ▸ Selected questions on running records
Questions or Prompts	▸ "Read out loud to me, please."	▸ "Retell the book to me. What happened first?" ▸ "What problem(s) is your character dealing with?" ▸ "Describe what you picture in this part." ▸ "Tell me about an important event. What causes it to happen?"	▸ "What ideas do you have about the character _____ ?" ▸ "How is your character feeling in this part?" ▸ "How is your character changing?" ▸ "Describe the relationship between _____ and _____ ." ▸ "How does [character] affect [character]?	▸ [identify a word or phrase with context support] "What does this mean?" ▸ "Can you explain what the word _____ means?"

Goal	COMPREHENSION: THEMES AND IDEAS	COMPREHENSION: MAIN IDEA	COMPREHENSION: KEY DETAILS	COMPREHENSION: TEXT FEATURES
Skills	‣ Interpreting messages and lessons ‣ Interpreting symbolism ‣ Interpreting social issues	‣ Synthesizing information to determine main idea(s) of parts and whole text	‣ Synthesizing key information to support main ideas ‣ Comparing and contrasting information	‣ Determining important information in text features and synthesizing it with information in the main text and in other features.
Assessments	‣ Whole-book assessment ‣ Conferring ‣ Selected questions on running records	‣ Whole-book assessment ‣ Conferring ‣ Selected questions on running records	‣ Whole-book assessment ‣ Conferring ‣ Selected questions on running records	‣ Whole-book assessment ‣ Conferring ‣ Selected questions on running records
Questions or Prompts	‣ "What is a lesson or message you can learn from this book?" ‣ "What does _____ symbolize?" ‣ "What social issues are coming up in this book?"	‣ "What is this book mostly about?" ‣ "What is this section mostly about?" ‣ "State a main idea for this section in your own words."	‣ "What details support the main idea you just said?" ‣ "It says here *[state main idea]*. What did you learn from this section that supports that?"	‣ "How does this *[feature]* add to what you're learning in this section?" ‣ "What are you learning from *[feature]*?"

	CONVERSATION	WRITING ABOUT READING
Goal		
Skills	▸ Speaking and listening skills, including disagreeing respectfully, sticking to a topic, and flexible thinking	▸ Short in-the-moment jots ▸ Longer, informal writing to explore thinking
Assessments	▸ Conversation transcript ▸ Conversation conference note-taking	▸ Sticky notes ▸ Reading notebook entries
Questions or Prompts	Observe students discussing books in pairs, small groups, and/or as a whole class. ▸ "How do you use your partnership / book club time to help you as a reader?"	Look at a student's writing about reading. ▸ "How do you decide when to write about your reading?" ▸ "How does writing about reading help you as a reader?"

Spotlight on EMERGENT BILINGUALS

Assessment

While it's true that students learn about language from reading (including vocabulary and the structure of language, for example), their reading abilities can also be impacted by their language abilities, so it's important to assess both.

▸ Oral Language surveys such as those that ask students to repeat back sentences of increasing complexity can help you learn about students' receptive language and their understanding of sentence structure.

▸ Mary Cappelini's (2005) language checklists and other assessments can help you determine stages of language acquisition to identify language goals for students who need them.

▸ Opitz and Guccione's (2009) Stages of Language Proficiency can be a helpful guide of what to look for.

Some scholars advocate for multilingual practices during formative assessment, by, for example, allowing students to respond to questions in their first language or by using a mixture of their home language and English. This can offer teachers a more complete picture of students' reading and language skills (Ascenzi-Moreno 2018).

How Do I Confer with a Reader When I Don't Know the Book?

It's understandable to feel uncertain or insecure when children might know more than you know about the book they are reading. As a consultant who models conferences and small groups in classrooms each week with kids and books I often don't know, I rely on a few guiding principles to help me assess a student and teach what they need most:

Guiding Principles

1. I worry less about the content of the book and focus instead on what I know about children's literature in general. I call on my knowledge of text complexity (Serravallo 2018; Fountas and Pinnell 2017), as well as what I know about genre.

2. I sometimes read a small bit of the book to ground me—I skim the blurb, peek at the cover, or even sneak a quick glance at the page the student is reading. I notice what I do as a reader, and compare that to what I notice the student doing.

3. Once students are working on a goal, I try to learn about the work they are doing related to their goal, rather than explore every possible area of reading. This helps narrow the focus and makes my decision making easier.

But perhaps what I rely on most is this adage: *Teach the reader, not the book.* I don't worry about whether every response students give me is exactly "right," and I focus more on the skills and strategies they are using within the book. My assessment of their reading work and the feedback and strategies I offer are based on what I hear and observe.

ASSESSMENT CONFERENCES
Structure and Timing

Part of the art of conducting an effective Assessment Conference is to ask questions in a way that feels like a conversation, rather than an inquisition. It's important, also, to remember that you're assessing what the *student can do*, not what the student can do with lots and lots of prompting, feedback, and support from a teacher. Try to stay disciplined about asking the question, and then stay quiet while assuming a listening stance. Try not to coach the child or to offer lots of feedback, response, or praise. Your job is to listen and analyze the responses a student offers, so you can figure out what area to pinpoint for a goal.

The Assessment Conference, which lasts about five to seven minutes, follows this structure:

Print your own table tent to have on hand during Assessment Conferences.

1 Prepare

Student brings their baggie of self-selected books.

2 Assess

Teacher asks the student questions and prompts them to talk about their reading life and/or reading work and to read aloud. The teacher can decide to assess all, or most, of the possible goal areas.

3 Compliment

Teacher gives the student a clear compliment (see more in Chapter 4) and sends the student off to continue their independent reading.

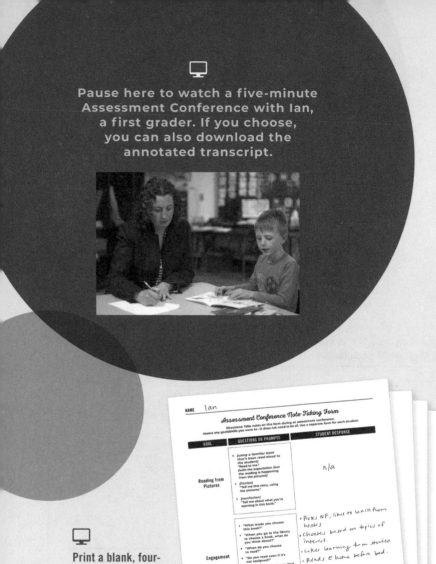

Pause here to watch a five-minute Assessment Conference with Ian, a first grader. If you choose, you can also download the annotated transcript.

Print a blank, four-page note-taking form that includes prompts to assess skills for each goal. Assess some or all possible goal areas. You can also go online to see my notes from my conference with Ian.

WATCH AND READ
An Assessment Conference Example

Here are some important teaching moves to notice in the conference:

▶ I try to keep prompts as open-ended as possible as my aim is to uncover what he is able to do independently, without much support from a teacher.

▶ I try to keep my questions brief and allow him to do much of the talking.

▶ After getting some information about his reading life and book choices, I transition to assess Print Work and Fluency.

▶ While he reads aloud, I take a quick running record, noting his fluency and accuracy. I record miscues, and, if they are self-corrected, what he does as a reader to make the correction.

▶ After a sample of his reading aloud, I move on to ask about comprehension. His book is fiction, so I stick with fiction goals: Plot and Setting, Character, and Themes and Ideas. I don't ask about Vocabulary, since the words in his book aren't challenging from a meaning perspective.

▶ My questions are appropriate for the level of complexity of his book.

▶ I end by giving him some positive feedback.

Finding a Goal

When reflecting on an Assessment Conference to figure out what goal to work on with a student, it's important to know what to expect. For example, if a student responds to the prompt "What ideas do you have about the character?" with "She's happy," that may show adequate comprehension or it may show the student needs to focus on a character goal. How do we know if the student's response is "good enough"? It comes down to what's in the text the student is reading and whether the response adequately captures its complexities. For a simple late-kindergarten or early-first-grade book, naming a single character feeling is likely enough. But for a fifth grader reading a 150-page novel, I'd worry that the student wasn't completely "getting it" with just one single word to describe the character.

As a teacher, it helps to get to know children's literature. I like to read several examples of books of the sort that my students will be reading. When I taught third grade, I read many different titles from books like *Poppleton*, all the way through books like *Because of Winn-Dixie*. I got to know familiar authors and series. I started to have an internalized sense of what the student could expect to encounter in books at each level and crafted my own ideas of what my "look-fors" would be from the students.

As a staff developer, I've been working with teachers to develop knowledge about expectations for reading skills and behaviors level by level. This is work you might do with your colleagues at professional learning community (PLC) or grade-level meetings. If you're interested in trying it, see the procedure we follow at right.

A procedure for studying texts:

▸ Before we meet, each teacher reads several books at whatever level(s) we decide to study together.

▸ Next, we meet to talk about supports and challenges in the texts, and what we'd expect of readers based on those challenges. We often consult resources such as Irene Fountas and Gay Su Pinnell's *The Fountas & Pinnell Literacy Continuum* (2017), Jan Richardson's *The Next Step Forward in Guided Reading* (2016), or my own *Understanding Texts & Readers* (2018).

▸ Finally, we create a simple chart like the one on pages 24–25 for each level to use as a reference.

EXAMPLE "LOOK-FOR" GUIDE (LEVEL I)

Engagement

▸ Sustain approximately 25+ minutes of independent reading.

▸ Read 12–15 books per week.

▸ Reread with purpose.

▸ Choose books based on interest.

Plot and Setting

▸ Retell with about five important events in sequence.

▸ Name where the story takes place, and identify changes in setting.

Print Work

▸ Read through longer words, word part by word part.

▸ Use pictures as a source of information.

▸ Integrate all three cueing systems: meaning, syntax, and visual.

▸ Use knowledge of irregular vowel patterns.

▸ Read known sight words automatically.

▸ Self-correct immediately, at or near the point of error.

▸ Pay attention to inflected endings (-*ed*, -*ing*, etc.) and contractions and read them accurately.

▸ Use a known word to read an unfamiliar word.

Character

▸ Name how characters feel based on text and pictures.

▸ Name a simple trait.

▸ Explain how character feelings change.

Fluency

▸ Read in long phrases (syntactically appropriate).

▸ Read with appropriate intonation and expression, reflecting dialogue versus narration, showing an understanding about not just what's said but how it's said.

Vocabulary and Figurative Language

▸ Infer the meaning of new vocabulary from pictures.

▸ In nonfiction, understand topic-related vocabulary. Pause in the text to figure out the meaning of the word, using text, glossary, and/or pictures. Provide a clear, complete definition in own words (not just reading from glossary definition).

Themes and Ideas

▸ Infer a lesson or message.

Main Idea

▸ Name the subtopics of each section (or page spread).

▸ Name the topic of the book in a sentence (it may not be the same as the title—the student needs to think about the information in the text).

▸ If the topic lends itself to ideas (e.g., "day and night"), say a simple idea about the topic.

Key Details

▸ List multiple facts that connect to each subtopic and be able to do this for several of the spreads or sections. Rely more on words than pictures to list facts.

Text Features

▸ Apply information from the main text to explain what the picture teaches.

Conversation

▸ Talk about what's in the text.

▸ Stay on topic.

▸ Take turns—one child's comment builds on the previous comment.

▸ Actively listen and paraphrase what another says.

▸ Ask questions to keep the conversation going.

▸ Make connections and elaborate on how the connections relate to the text.

Writing About Reading

▸ Jot occasionally to record reactions, thoughts, or feelings of characters, or to mark pages the student intends to discuss with a partner or teacher.

Now, reflect on the conference I had with Ian. Consider what he demonstrated he was able to do, and compare it to the chart of expectations for what Engagement, Print Work, Fluency, and the various comprehension goals look like for books at the level he's reading. Can you identify an area where you feel like he could use some support to grow?

MY THOUGHTS

Given his responses to my questions, I think a good goal for him would be to better understand the Plot and Setting. Specifically, I think he could use some support with retelling the events of the stories he reads. It's interesting to me that he seems to gravitate toward nonfiction (which is often written with an expository, nonnarrative structure). Even when reading fiction, he notes that he likes to learn lessons. In fact, the lesson he inferred was quite impressive! Focusing more on the events and how the events connect could help him with comprehension. I think that Ian is a big-picture thinker, and he could use support with the details. Since he demonstrated strengths in all other areas, I would bet that he'd be able to start trying more challenging books after a few weeks with this goal.

In the online resources you will find a sample "Look-For" chart and the blank template shown above that you can use to create your own charts.

{ *Take It to*
YOUR CLASSROOM

Here is some advice for how you can incorporate Assessment Conferences into your classroom:

✓

Consider downloading the Assessment Conference note-taking forms. Use them to remind you of questions and prompts to ask readers to learn more about what they already know and do for each of the thirteen possible goal categories. If you decide to use them, make multiple copies so you have one for each student. 🖥

✓

Try to spend five to ten minutes with each student in your class getting to know them as readers. You may decide to check in to see how they are doing with each possible goal, or you may focus only on select goals. For example, if you just conducted formal running records (using the *Fountas & Pinnell Benchmark Assessment System* or something similar), you may decide you don't need to listen to students read aloud again to check for Fluency or Print Work (Fountas and Pinnell 2016, 2017).

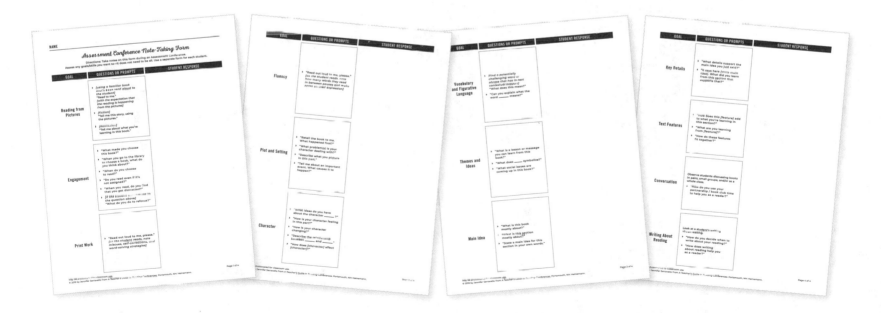

Mentor Spotlight
MARIE CLAY

Marie Clay's methods for observing children and tailoring instruction to individuals have influenced decades of reading instruction. Clay developed Running Records, an assessment used to document student reading of continuous text to determine text appropriateness and possibilities for teaching. Running Records is one of six tasks in the Observation Survey considered the gold standard of literacy assessment that can be used with five- to seven-year-olds in any setting. As well, she developed the highly regarded Reading Recovery intervention designed to support first-grade students not getting underway well with reading and writing. Not only is the design of the intervention remarkable, but so too is the insistence that teachers who deliver it undergo consistent, ongoing professional learning to deeply understand reading and writing development. This may be one of the things I love about Clay most: she believes a knowledgeable teacher is among the most powerful gifts we can give young readers.

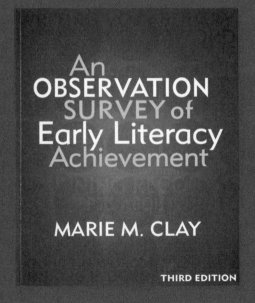

My advice: Start your reading here

{ A Few Favorite Words About Assessment from Marie Clay }

" *The teacher may teach thirty children in his or her class, but the learning takes place in each individual differently. Instruction needs to meet an individual learner on a personalized level whenever the learning is challenging for that student.* (31)

Clay, Marie M. 2014. *By Different Paths to Common Outcomes.* Portsmouth, NH: Heinemann.

I believe so strongly that every child is unique and individual, and that we have to match our instruction to each. There is a place for whole-class instruction, but most of the time we should work with kids individually and/or in small groups. And even when kids are in small groups, it's still important to give individual feedback.

And then all these wise words from the Clay classic, *An Observation Survey* (1993):

> *To use systematic observation the teacher has to set time aside from teaching to become a neutral observer.* (1)

I love this quote because it reminds me that the part of teaching where we stop talking and take time to listen and watch is so important. The information a teacher gets from backing up, quieting down, and watching what students can do is so valuable.

> *Teachers should always leave room to be surprised by individual children.* (4)

As teachers, we're often working with some theory of who kids are as learners and as people, but it's important to always keep an open mind in assessment: to explore more than just those things that would confirm what we already think and to be open to seeing new things—including that a student may suddenly be able to do something they weren't able to do just a day ago!

> *By comparison with the observation of learners at work, test scores are mere approximations or estimates, at times misrepresenting individual progress in learning, and at times presenting results stripped of the very information that is required for designing or evaluating sound instruction.* (1–2)

Clay wrote this in 1993, but it's relevant today as standardized tests, and standardized progress monitoring, become more and more commonplace and high stakes. Teachers need to be empowered to use real classroom data (observations, informal records, etc.) to understand how students are growing and to know what to teach next.

> *All [children] are ready to learn, but are starting from different places . . . it is the teachers who need to know how to create appropriate instruction for where each child is.* (6)

A reminder that "all children are ready" is so important when we assess so we don't focus on deficits or what kids *can't* do. Instead, we focus on strengths first, and teaching opportunities that are next steps from those strengths.

chapter three

SETTING *Goals*

Deciding on a Goal Together

Once you've spent time assessing—either by looking at student work, conducting formal assessments, and/or doing an Assessment Conference—you'll have an idea of the goal that will most benefit each student. While it's tempting just to tell them ("You need to work on understanding plot and setting. Let's start practicing retelling!"), students will be more engaged when they have a say in their goals. Imposing goals can also cause students to become compliant but not as intrinsically motivated (see, for example, Pink 2011; Schlechty 2001; Hattie 2008). Knowing this, it may be tempting to simply say to children, "Pick a goal that you think you want to work on." However, if students choose something random, without any guidance or reflection, they may come up with superficial goals such as "I want to read bigger books" or "I want to read faster." Also, in many cases, kids may just say something they think we want to hear.

Guiding students to set meaningful, ambitious goals begins with teachers inviting readers to reflect on their work, their strengths, and where they can grow. There are many ways to begin this guided reflection. Some teachers gather the class for a brief lesson in which they introduce each of the possible goals from the hierarchy (page 14) and ask students to think, or maybe jot, about which goal feels most important to them. Other teachers like to ask children to do some quiet self-reflection, perhaps with a questionnaire (see "What Can I Work On as a Reader?", at right). Still others choose to sit one-on-one with students to guide them to reflect on a specific sample of their work. No matter how you guide students to reflect, remember that both reflection and guidance are key to helping students establish their goals. As the expert in the room, you may need to steer students back on track if their interpretation of their work is off base.

INVITE STUDENTS TO REFLECT

I recommend offering students some time to reflect regularly on their reading, their thinking, and their writing about reading, especially before you plan to meet with them in a Goal-Setting Conference. For students in upper elementary through middle school, a self-reflection questionnaire may be helpful (see example at right). Students can read the statements aligned to goals and reflect on the ones they feel are always true, sometimes true, or never true. In the primary grades, this tool could be used as a list of questions you ask students during the conference, or questions you could pose to the class to help them with their independent reflections. You can download your own copy from the online resources.

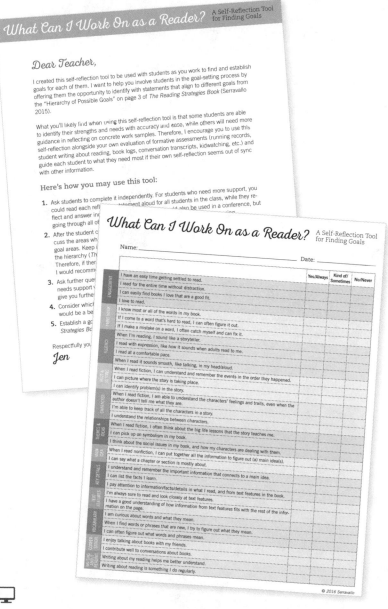

Download your own copy of the "What Can I Work On as a Reader?" form.

Goal Setting

Based on your assessments, students may have a *language* goal they are working on alongside their *reading* goal. The language goals might be connected to vocabulary, features of language such as tenses or sentence structure, or communicating ideas both orally and in writing.

Preparing for a Goal-Setting Conference

To engage students in meaningful self-reflection, it's important to have concrete examples of their work at hand. Based on my assessment, I ask students to bring, or I will prepare, some things for us to look at together. So as not to overwhelm students, I select only the work that will help them focus on strengths and the possibilities for next steps. Here are some examples of the kinds of things I might gather, depending on the goal I've noticed a student is likely to need support with.

The student needs to work toward . . .	Sorts of work I'd ask the student to bring (or I'd gather) . . .
Better understanding characters, including inferring about main and secondary characters, and having ideas about character relationships	▸ Sticky notes that show thinking about characters ▸ Writing about reading in the child's reading notebook that shows minimal thinking about characters ▸ A sample rubric or description of the kinds of thinking readers can do about characters ▸ A conversation transcript of the student and peers
Improving accuracy by using print work skills such as: decoding by reading through the whole word, monitoring for meaning, catching errors, and self-correcting	A running record showing the student's miscues and the text the student read

Materials to Prepare for a Goal-Setting Conference, continued

The student needs to work toward . . .	Sorts of work I'd ask the student to bring (or I'd gather) . . .
Summarizing the most important key details from a nonfiction text by connecting information to the main idea	▸ Written summaries of nonfiction books ▸ A conversation transcript of the student and peers discussing a nonfiction text ▸ A sample rubric showing summaries that range in quality from more simplistic to more sophisticated
Improving fluency by phrasing in ways that are meaningful and by using more expression and intonation	▸ A fluency record (an excerpt of text with slash marks indicating each place where the reader paused) ▸ An audio recording of the student reading aloud

GOAL-SETTING CONFERENCES
Structure and Timing

The Goal-Setting Conference lasts about five minutes and follows a predictable structure:

1 Guided inquiry

Lead the student through reflection using a self-assessment questionnaire and/or teacher-selected work samples.

🖵
Print your own table tent to have on hand during Goal-Setting Conferences.

GOAL-SETTING Conference
(5 minutes)

1 Guided inquiry (2 minutes)
Lead the student through reflection using a self-assessment questionnaire and/or teacher-selected work samples.

2 Name the goal (<30 seconds)
Together, name the goal. Feel free to use kid-friendly language or one of the goal terms in the hierarchy (page 14). The goal should be something ambitious the student will work toward (with support, strategies, and feedback) over several weeks.

3 Teach (<30 seconds)
Offer the student a strategy so that after the conference, they may begin working toward the goal.

4 Coach (2 minutes)
Support the student as they practice.

5 Link (<30 seconds)
Repeat the goal and strategy and offer the student a visible reminder of both.

2 Name the goal

Together, name the goal. Feel free to use kid-friendly language or one of the goal terms in the hierarchy (page 14). The goal should be something ambitious the student will work toward (with support and feedback) for several weeks.

4 Coach

Support the student as they practice.

3 Teach

Offer the student a strategy so that after the conference, they may begin working toward the goal.

5 Link

Repeat the goal and strategy, and offer the student a visible reminder of both.

What's a Strategy?

The word *strategy* is used in different ways by different researchers, authors, and theorists (Keene and Zimmerman 2007; Afflerbach, Pearson, and Paris 2008; Harvey and Goudvis 2007; Wiggins 2013; Beers 2002). I use the term to refer to a *how-to*, while the goal that a student is working toward is the *what*. Strategies, like a recipe, offer students a broken-down, step-by-step procedure that makes the invisible work of reading actionable and visible. Strategies are introduced and practiced, and then eventually they fade away as the student develops automaticity.

See one example of a goal with related skills and strategies at the right. For more strategies, see *The Reading Strategies Book* (Serravallo 2015).

GOAL
(Fluency)

SKILL
(Phrasing)

SKILL
(Intonation and Expression)

STRATEGY
(Look ahead in the sentence for punctuation that tells you when to pause, such as commas, dashes, and semicolons. Read up to the punctuation, take a short break, and then read the next group of words.)

STRATEGY
(Warm up with phrases that show up often in books. When you see the phrases in your book, read them without pausing.)

STRATEGY
(When there is dialogue, make sure you think about what's being said, how the character says it, and what the character's feeling. When the character stops talking, change your voice to sound like the narrator.)

STRATEGY
(Pay attention to ending punctuation. Look ahead to the end of the sentence. Notice if there is an exclamation point, question mark, or period. Make your voice match the punctuation.)

WATCH AND READ
A Goal-Setting Conference Example

Pause here to watch an example of a Goal-Setting Conference with a fifth grader, Gavin, or, if you prefer, download the annotated transcript.

The conference follows the typical flow of a Goal-Setting Conference, so try to identify the five stages as you watch. Here are some teaching moves to notice in the conference:

▶ I start the conference by asking Gavin what he's already doing as a reader, and then I give him a quick overview of the kinds of thinking (represented by goals) he might be doing.

▶ Gavin is using his reader's notebook to help him reflect on his thinking. Notice that I am looking at the notebook with him, and I often point out things I see that support what he's saying.

▶ Wait time is critical during guided inquiry. Notice the number of times I remain silent to give Gavin time to think.

▶ More than once, I ask Gavin to extend his thinking: "What else do you notice?"

▶ Often, I "say back" what I'm hearing to make sure I'm understanding or to name the work that Gavin is doing: "So it sounds like you are . . ."

▶ When Gavin says he wants to work on "Themes and Ideas," I ask, "What makes you say that?" Follow-up questions like this prompt students to think about why they are making decisions.

▶ Notice the number of times I remind Gavin that this is just the *beginning* of his work on this goal. This language helps students understand that goals are something they will work on over time.

▶ As we record the goal, I am careful to distinguish between the goal and the strategy, an important difference.

Get a close-up look at my notes from this conference in the online resources, where you can also find blank conferring forms for each goal, complete with skill progressions and sample research questions, to offer you support as you confer with your readers.

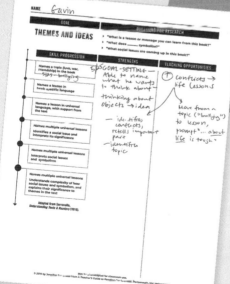

Making Goals Visible

As you confer with your students to establish goals and offer strategies that match their strengths and needs, you'll need some system for keeping each reader organized and focused. Just as you have classroom charts that chronicle the goals and strategies you offer during whole-class instruction, students also need visible tools and reminders of their personal goals to use during their independent practice time.

Whether you use a bookmark, dedicate a page in each student's reader's notebook, or create a page that slips into a book baggie or reading folder, it's important that you build the tool you offer with the student over time. While you could easily download a premade bookmark off the Internet with a list of six Print Work strategies, the bookmark will likely go unused since it wasn't created with the student during guided practice. The pictures don't need to be Pinterest-worthy; just make something on the spot. You might jot key words, simple steps, or maybe even a quick picture sketch to remind the student of what you worked on together and what they should continue trying on their own.

 One teacher uses a half page of bright-colored cardstock for each student. During independent practice time she signals students: "Take out your orange goal cards, and as you read today, remember what you're working on as a reader." This cue offers students a helpful transition from whole-class unit-focused work to work on their individual goals. A blank of this bookmark is available online.

 A first-grade teacher has her students keep a one-page form in their reading folders. Notice that students often transition to new goals after about four weeks. The strategy reminders (in the boxes below the goal box) are added during conferences. A blank of this form is available online.

A kindergarten teacher divides a page in half: half for strategies the student is currently practicing, and half for strategies that have become habit. Students move the sticky notes from left to right as they feel the strategy has become automatic.

A fourth-grade teacher invites students to teach others through student-led sign-up seminars. Once students feel comfortable with their goal-directed learning, other students can sign up to learn from the expert.

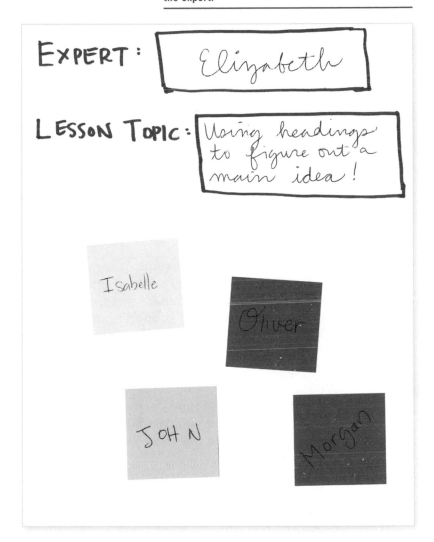

A Close-Up Look at Guided Inquiry

Understanding guided inquiry is important to your ability to successfully conduct a Goal-Setting Conference. Ideally, the questions you ask students will be open-ended enough to allow them to reflect and understand something about their work, and then arrive at goals that will help them grow as readers.

As the expert in the room, the teacher plays an important role, guiding students to notice things about their reading habits and skills and mentoring them as they develop their reading lives. This is why I use the term *guided* inquiry. It's inquiry because you are asking questions and looking for students to reflect, respond, and draw conclusions, but you are guiding them to see what goals would benefit them. Just remember: helping students realize their goals increases their agency and ownership.

Of course, there are times when students draw conclusions about their work that are slightly different than what you hoped they'd say. For example, perhaps you're hoping a student decides they could use some support understanding vocabulary when they read nonfiction. But during the conference, it becomes clear that they often ignore text features. The student reflects that perhaps if they studied text features more closely, they'd better understand the content. In a situation like that, if their line of thinking makes sense, and especially if their goal will also help with what I had originally identified as a need, I'd shift gears, be flexible, and honor their goal choice.

There are other times when students have a very hard time seeing what would benefit them most as readers. For example, if you have a student who reads one word at a time, haltingly, without much expression, then Fluency seems the obvious focus. However, let's say the student wants to work on understanding Plot and Setting. If you feel strongly that they need to work on Fluency, you can have them compare their work against others or the expectation. In this Fluency example, I might read a sample of text to the child to show them how it sounds when they read, and then reread the same sample fluently and ask if they can hear a difference.

A child working on a comprehension goal might benefit from seeing a learning progression, like those in *Reading Pathways*, which is included with Lucy Calkins' *Units of Study for Teaching Reading, Grades K–5* (2015), or those in *Understanding Texts & Readers* (Serravallo 2018). A student who needs support with their conversational skills might benefit from watching a video of a skilled partnership or book club and being prompted to name the differences they see between the exemplar and their own practice. While showing exemplars can offer students tremendous clarity, it's important that this is done with sensitivity and compassion, so students don't feel bad about their own work. I find it helps to point out for children how the work they are currently doing is an "almost" version of the exemplar and show them some ways I'll offer support as they work toward their goal.

"What do you notice about your work?"

"What do you think you're doing well as a reader?"

"What do you think you might want to work on?"

"One thing I notice is _____. What are your thoughts?"

"Can you think of ways that I can help you grow as a reader?"

"Look at _____. Compare it to what you're doing as a reader."

"What is some new work you may want to take on?"

"Can you think of any ways you may want to improve or deepen your thinking about the books you're reading?"

"Is there anything you notice from this [rubric, student sample, exemplar] that you'd like to work on?"

"What's going to make the biggest difference for you as a reader?"

{ *Take It to* YOUR CLASSROOM

Here is some practical advice for having conversations with students about the work they want to take on as readers, while putting them in the driver's seat of the decision making:

✓ Think about what you know about your readers from your assessments, including your Assessment Conferences. When you meet with each student, be prepared with a sample of their work that will help each student see what you saw.

✓ In the goal-setting conference you watched with Gavin, I introduced the goals to him while I was working with him one-on-one. To save time, you might

▸ Introduce the possible goals to your whole class, all at once. Then, give students time to self-reflect before meeting with them in a Goal-Setting Conference.

▸ Use the "What Can I Work On as a Reader?" self-reflection to get students thinking about what goal(s) might be a good fit for them.

▸ Combine the Assessment Conference and Goal-Setting Conference into one meeting with each student. After assessing the student, ask them to reflect on which of the questions you asked and the tasks you asked them to do (reading aloud, for example) were most challenging, and have the student set a goal from there, right there.

✓ Take notes on what you discuss and work on with each student, and leave the student with a physical reminder of your conversation. This will help ensure children are set up to practice independently, holds them accountable to continue practicing the strategy, and helps you remember what to follow up on next time.

Mentor Spotlight
JOHN HATTIE

John Hattie is the author of the groundbreaking book *Visible Learning* (2008), which documents his meta-analysis of thousands of educational studies in a quest to find out which educational practices have the greatest impact on student achievement. His research helps educators make more informed decisions, and my work has been heavily influenced by his findings. Hattie is an important researcher to follow as he's constantly updating his work with a review of the most current studies. Some of his more recent publications include *Visible Learning into Action* (Hattie, Masters, and Birch 2015), *Visible Learning Feedback* (Hattie and Clarke 2018), and *Teaching Literacy in the Visible Learning Classroom* (Fisher, Frey, and Hattie 2017). He agreed to answer a few of my questions about his research that relate to goal setting with students.

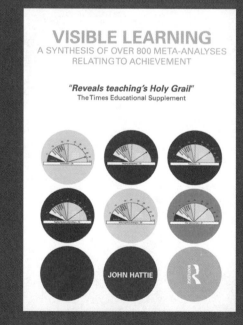

My advice: Start your reading here

JEN: Your work helping teachers understand what educational practices have the biggest impact on student growth is earth-shattering. What do you hope educators most understand about this work?

JOHN HATTIE: The evidence in *Visible Learning* relates to "probabilities" about the impact of various interventions, and one core notion is that the evidence helps educators choose high-probability intervention strategies. The second core notion is that educators need to evaluate their interventions to know their impact: Know thy impact. This begs the moral purpose question as to what you mean by impact (and I hope it is more than achievement but certainly includes achievement), whom did you impact, and to what magnitude.

JEN: What would you say is most important for teachers to understand about the role of goal setting and teacher clarity?

JOHN HATTIE: Starting from a decent needs analysis of what students already know, can do, and care about; working with them to set goals (we use the term *personal bests*) that are not too hard and not too boring; and then providing instruction to close the gap between where they are and where we want them to be, smelling the roses of the success of this learning, and then reinvesting in more learning via the next success criteria.

JEN: What is most important to know about student self-reflection and self-directed learning?

JOHN HATTIE: Student control over learning is close to zero impact—all of us need experts (teachers, books, others) to stretch us to new territories—what Vygotsky termed the zone of proximal development. The self-reflection therefore needs to be more about the "how" we get there, the optimal strategies we have (and maybe need), and the skills to direct (which include skills to seek help, wallow in errors and see them as opportunities, and work with others). More often we learn best when we work with others who can help us see ourselves "from the other side of the mirror."

JEN: Can you explain "teacher efficacy," something you've found to have an enormous effect size, and what it means in the classroom?

JOHN HATTIE: The collective confidence of a group of educators that they *can* cause learning, have high expectations, and continue to debate what a year's growth for a year's input means—*fed* with the evidence of impact. This can triple the rate of student learning—it requires a great leader, high levels of social sensitivity, and the deep commitment to making the difference together.

JEN: What's the most misinterpreted practice among those at the top of your effect size list? What do teachers need to understand about it?

JOHN HATTIE: Feedback—it is powerful but among the most variable. About a third of feedback can be negative. Working out the conditions of optimal feedback has been a fifteen-year journey, and Shirley Clarke and I have just released our book on this topic.

chapter four

NOTICING AND NAMING
Strengths

Feedback can offer students corrections, critiques, or praise. Feedback that is highly effective should be specific and clear, elaborated upon, focused on the task rather than the learner, as simple as possible, supportive, timely, and connected to the goal (Shute 2007; Brophy 1981; Hattie 2008; Wiggins 2012). In this chapter, the focus will be on reinforcing strategies students are already using by offering helpful praise in what I call Compliment Conferences (Serravallo and Goldberg 2007).

Not all praise is created equally. Alfie Kohn (1999) has been quite vocal about problems associated with praise, in fact. Kohn writes, "The more we say, 'I like the way you . . . ' or 'Good _____ing,' the more kids come to rely on *our* evaluations, *our* decisions about what's good and bad, rather than learning to form their own judgments. It leads them to measure their worth in terms of what will lead *us* to smile and dole out some more approval" (2001 [italics added]). Instead of telling students "good job," Kohn advises us to "say what you saw."

Peter Johnston (2004) calls "saying what you saw," *noticing and naming*. He argues that we should name for students their approximations toward their goals and name explicitly what we see, something Marie Clay (1993a) calls attending to the "partially correct." Carol Dweck (2006), known for her groundbreaking work on growth versus fixed mindsets, argues that positive feedback should be focused on effort, rather than ability. In fact, she found that "when students were praised for effort, 90% of them wanted the challenging new task they could learn from" (72).

The Anatomy of an Effective Compliment

Taking my cues from Hattie, Kohn, Dweck, Johnston, and Clay, when complimenting readers I aim to be as precise as possible, and I try to leave off the "I love the ways" and the "Goods" and "Great jobs" (though admittedly, I still sometimes slip). My mentor Kathleen Tolan used to say that a helpful compliment is a "paragraph of speech."

A compliment structure:

▶ Name the strategy the student is using.

▶ Explain why that strategy is helpful and/or will help with the student's reading goal.

▶ Refer to an example of something the student said or wrote or did when reading aloud (when needed).

Instead of complimenting the reader like this . . .	Try to offer specific feedback like this . . .
"Your reading sounds so great!"	"I notice that your pauses match the punctuation. For example, here where there is a comma in the middle of the sentence, I heard you read it like this. [Read it back, pausing at the comma.] Reading in phrases will help you chunk the sentence in meaningful ways."
"What a smart idea you wrote on the sticky note."	"It seems like you stopped in a place where the character surprised you, and you took time to jot a quick idea you had about the character in that moment. When you're paying attention to moments like these, it'll help you see that characters are not just one way, just like people in real life."
"You got all the words right!"	"With this word [point], and again with this word [point], you slowed down to figure out what they were. I saw you break the word up, part by part, then blend all the parts together, moving from left to right. That helped you approach a long word that you didn't recognize right away."
"You're working hard to stay focused today."	"I was watching you from across the classroom, and I could see that a few times during independent reading you got distracted. Each time, you turned back a page and reread to jump back into your reading. It seems like that really helped you to refocus and reengage with your reading."

Spotlight on
EMERGENT BILINGUALS

Supporting Growing Language Skills

▸ It's crucial for all children, but especially those learning in a new language, to build confidence. Noticing student strengths, when done in a genuine way, helps to do that and also helps build trust between teacher and student.

▸ When conferring, in addition to complimenting students on reading skills, you might also compliment them on their growing language skills. Listen for children's use of new vocabulary; their ability to explain, retell, label, describe; or use a new sentence structure or tense in their speaking or writing.

COMPLIMENT CONFERENCES
Structure and Timing

Compliment conferences are short—usually under two minutes each. In the first part of the conference (the *research*), I quickly try to learn about the work the student is doing connected to their goal. I don't assess everything; I focus. If the student's goal is Print Work or Fluency, I will ask them to read aloud. If the student's goal is comprehension based, I'll usually ask questions and/or look at the student's writing about reading. If the child is working on Engagement, I might discuss their book choices, look at a reading log, or spend some time observing them as they read. I listen closely during this research and notice what the student is working toward, attempting, and approximating. I decide on something to name, and then I offer a compliment in a paragraph's worth of feedback (described earlier).

Print your own table tent to have on hand during Compliment Conferences.

1 Research

Ask questions, observe, look at student work, and/or listen to the student read aloud.

2 Decide

Choose one strategy the student is using (or approximating).

3 Compliment

Offer the student elaborated feedback (what the student did, why that's helpful, and perhaps an example).

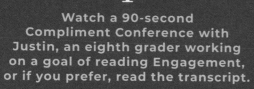

Watch a 90-second Compliment Conference with Justin, an eighth grader working on a goal of reading Engagement, or if you prefer, read the transcript.

Get a close-up look at my notes from this conference in the online resources, where you can also find blank conferring forms for each goal, complete with skill progressions and sample research questions, to offer you support as you confer with your readers.

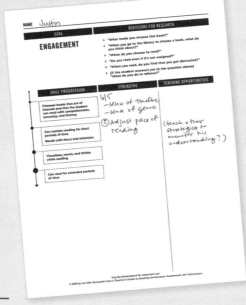

WATCH AND READ
A Compliment Conference Example

Justin is learning strategies for monitoring his own engagement and comprehension in a book and really trying to tune in to content. He's also working on reading stamina and being able to read for longer stretches. Here are a few teaching moves to notice in the short conference:

▶ I start by checking to see if he's monitoring his own comprehension because I notice the book he's reading looks challenging, which may be an obstacle to his ability to engage with the text.

▶ "How" questions ("Are you finding that there's any difference with the pace that you're reading this versus how you read, say, a fiction book?") are designed to help students name their own processes. When a student is able to name a specific strategy, that's often what I choose to compliment.

▶ I make a connection to Justin when I tell him I do the same thing he is doing as a reader. Connections like this build powerful relationships with students over time and develop a reader-to-reader mentorship.

▶ Notice that I offer feedback that is both generalizable and process oriented. Adjusting reading pace based on genre is something he can do not only with this book but with books in the future. I also explain why it's helpful (more information on each page means more to digest).

{ *Take It to* YOUR CLASSROOM

Here is some practical advice for integrating Compliment Conferences into your classroom:

During planning or collaborative study time, practice crafting compliments that are specific, clear, and free of words like *I love* and *Great* and *Good job*. It's incredible how easily these words slip out, even for someone who has been aware of the research against using them for more than a decade (me!).

Consider spending an entire reading period just giving positive feedback. It'll help you tune in to students' strengths and give you the chance to practice repeatedly. Also, I think you'll find that students appreciate their efforts being noticed in this way and your hour will be filled with smiles.

Take notes on what you discuss with each student. As you reinforce a strategy the student *is* using, you may also have ideas about what you might teach next (in a conference or small group). I sometimes jot down the compliment on the left-hand side of my notes and possible next steps on the right-hand side. Download your own conferring note-taking forms. 🖥

Mentor Spotlight
PETER JOHNSTON

You know those books you return to at different phases in your life? The ones you reread, and because you're coming to them with new life experiences, you are able to find more or think differently? *Catcher in the Rye. Charlotte's Web.*

Choice Words (2004) by Peter Johnston.

I have returned to this gem of a book many times. It's slim hundred-page length is deceptive—there is never a shortage of advice to carry away from it. The book lives within reach on my shelf, and Johnston's words live in my heart and mind each time I speak to a student.

Here are just a few lines that hopefully will entice you to grab your own copy of this book about how our language choices affect children's learning. These lines are teasers—Johnston unpacks each assertion with rich discussion, research, and classroom examples that will deepen your understandings in important ways.

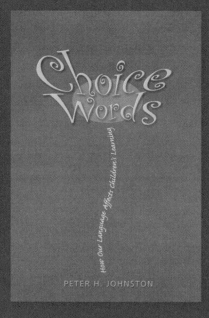

My advice: Start your reading here

> **Confirm what has been successful (so that it will be repeated) and simultaneously assert the learner's competence so she will have the confidence to consider near learning.** (13)

> **Focusing on the positive is hardly a new idea. It is just hard to remember to do it sometimes, particularly when the child's response is nowhere near what you expected.** (13)

> **"I'm proud of you," like other forms of praise, turns a child's attention to pleasing the teacher, rather than developing agency. . . . It also subtly removes some of the responsibility for the accomplishment and gives it to the teacher.** (25)

> **Teachers' conversations with children help the children build the bridges between action and consequence that develop their sense of agency. They show children how, by acting strategically, they accomplish things, and at the same time, that they are the kind of person who accomplishes things.** (30)

Noticing student strengths, when done in a genuine way, helps build a student's confidence, and the trust between a teacher and a student.

chapter five

Teaching Strategies
TO INDIVIDUALS AND GROUPS

As students work on their goals, they'll need guided practice with strategies. Coaching Conferences, Research-Compliment-Teach Conferences, and Strategy Lessons are ways to offer new strategies to students, help them practice strategies they've already learned, and monitor progress toward their goals.

Building on Strengths

When we offer students strategies, it's important to make sure we are considering their strengths *within* their goal. Building on strengths allows you to "build on student's knowledge, skills, and experiences . . . rather than chastise them for what they don't know" (Ladson-Billings 2009, 135). Building on strengths ensures you're working within students' zones of proximal development (Vygostsky 1978), that they have control of task difficulty (Allington

2011), and that they are likely to have some independence with the new strategy after a small amount of instruction and coaching from you.

When you're looking for strengths and next steps, it can be helpful to think of a continuum of skills within each goal. For example, it's not that students do or don't think about characters, or that they do or don't have fluency, but instead that their work within their goal falls somewhere along a progression.

Expectations for student work within a goal should also be considered within the context of the level of text they are reading (recall the "look-for" guide for Level I, pages 24–25).

Here's an example of a progression I created based on the 2002 NAEP fluency scale (Daane et al. 2005):

Reads word by word

Reads in two- to three-word phrases

Reads in longer phrases, though phrasing may be awkward

Reads in longer phrases, informed by midsentence punctuation (commas, dashes, semicolons)

Reads with appropriate phrasing and some expression, mostly informed by ending punctuation

Reads with appropriate phrasing and consistently uses expression that matches the author's meaning

Download goal-based conferring note-taking forms, each with their own progression of skills, for use in your conferences.

With this progression in mind, I can think about a student who needs support with fluency, place their reading somewhere along this continuum, look ahead to the right to see what's next, and teach a strategy for that. For example, if I am listening to a student reading and notice they're reading word by word, I'd start with teaching them to scoop up a couple of words at a time (unless the student is reading books at levels A and B, where one-to-one matching is first practiced and word-by-word reading should be expected). A student who is using occasional expression would next learn a strategy for using it more consistently.

Here's another example, considering a comprehension goal: understanding Characters. This progression is informed by my writing about comprehension in *Complete Comprehension* (2019) and *Understanding Texts & Readers* (2018). If you don't have these resources you can also take a look at the *Reading Pathways* book included in Lucy Calkins' *Units of Study for Reading, Grades K–5* (2015), or Irene Fountas and Gay Su Pinnell's *The Fountas & Pinnell Literacy Continuum* (2017).

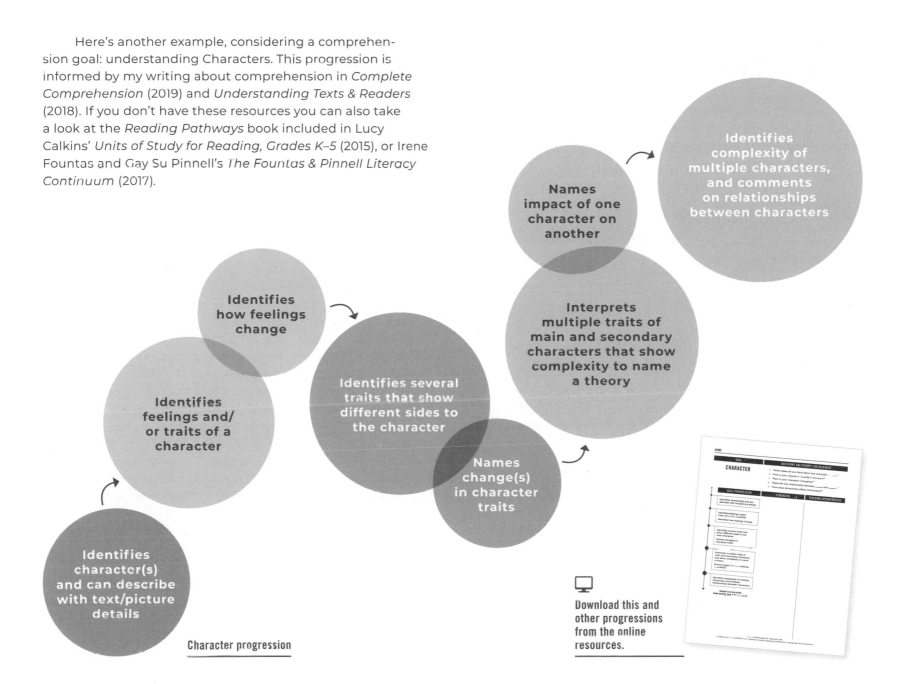

Character progression

Download this and other progressions from the online resources.

{ *Try It*
SCENARIO A

Have a go at this. Using the progression for understanding Character on page 59, what might you do with a student reading books around levels R, S, and T whose conference begins like this?

....

TEACHER: What ideas are you having about your character?

STUDENT: I think my character is nice and friendly.

....

What is this student doing well? What might you teach?

{ *Try It*
SCENARIO B

Have a look at another child's responses to some questions. She's reading books at levels J, K, and L. Think about what you'd do in this case:

....

TEACHER: What are you thinking about your character?

STUDENT: Well, I think she was feeling really lonely.

TEACHER: Has that changed?

STUDENT: She's starting to make some friends, but she wants to make more, so I'm not really sure.

....

What is this student doing well? What might you teach?

ONE TEACHER'S DECISION MAKING

For Scenario A, you may have noticed that the reader was able to name two similar traits (nice, friendly) using somewhat simplistic language. I might try to support the child with lists of character traits and a strategy for figuring out other words to use when describing the character.

For Scenario B, you may have noticed that the student was tuned in to a character feeling (lonely). With prompting, she was also thinking a bit about how the character is changing. She's not yet able to name the change, but she is picking up on important details that could help her infer that change. In this situation, I might work with her on naming feelings of the character at key points across the book, which would help her see changes in character feelings.

I don't want to suggest that reading is as linear and lockstep as the progressions I've shared may suggest: it's not. There may be reasons, for example, for a student working on Fluency to skip over reading in longer phrases in favor of practicing intonation and expression. For a child with a goal of understanding Character, you could choose to work on naming traits before tackling changes in characters' feelings. In general, though, I think it's so helpful to give some thought to how students can grow *within* goals so that we have some sense of what work may lie ahead and what the logical next steps are. If we don't do this, the results can be stalled decision making, lack of clarity for kids, and teaching that is less focused than it could be.

For more sample within-goal progressions, see the conferring note-taking forms in the online resources. 🖥

▶ Be sure to meet with these students as frequently or more frequently than others in the class. Keep their language goals and reading goals in mind and remember to build on strengths.

▶ You can affirm and extend approximations of language as you confer. For example, when a student points to a picture in a book and says, "Tree, big!" you might respond, "Yes, that tree is big!" Let your feedback model the structure of the language while affirming and reinforcing the student's approximation.

▶ Be sure to leave extra conferring time for students who are learning English to think, process, and understand what you say.

▶ Be as precise and clear with your language as possible.

▶ If you're offering a new strategy, provide students with a visual sketch and/or key words on their own sticky note to remind them of what they worked on with you.

▶ Consider a student's home language a strength, and offer them the chance to respond to your prompts and questions using their full linguistic repertoire (Ascenzi-Moreno 2018).

Providing Feedback and Coaching Readers

Offering students feedback and support happens in all conferences. As you may remember, at the end of the Assessment Conference with Ian, I offered him feedback on some of his strengths. In the Goal-Setting Conference with Gavin, after setting a goal and teaching a new strategy, I stuck around and gave him some support and feedback as he practiced. The Compliment Conference is all about offering targeted, positive feedback. So, as you now learn more about feedback and coaching readers, please apply what you understand to *all* conferring, and even consider rereading Chapters 2 through 4, or at least the conference transcripts, with these new understandings in mind.

Coaching Conferences and Research-Compliment-Teach Conferences have been written about extensively as helpful structures for working with individuals as they practice reading and writing strategies (Calkins 2000; Calkins, Hartman, and White 2005; Anderson 2000, 2018; Ray and Glover 2011; Serravallo and Goldberg 2007), as have small-group Strategy Lessons (Calkins 2000; Serravallo 2010). Because these types of conferences are about guiding and supporting children *as* they practice, feedback is crucial to their success. When you are working with students, you can catch them the moment they stumble, help them change course if they are going astray, and point out what they're doing that's working.

PROMPT TYPES

You can offer students coaching, support, and feedback during a conference in a variety of ways. Each has a slightly different purpose and offers slightly different types of support. Understanding these differences allows you to be flexible and responsive. For example, when a child has improved their fluency by paying attention to midsentence punctuation for the first time, I would want to reinforce this with a compliment prompt. However, if the only way I ever prompt is with directives, then that moment would likely pass unnoticed.

Type of Prompt or Feedback	DIRECTIVE	REDIRECTION	QUESTION
Purpose	To ask the student to do something specific.	To point out what the reader is doing and how what I'm prompting for is slightly different.	To prompt the reader to try something or to get the reader to self-reflect.
Example	▸ "Check the picture." ▸ "Reread that and see how it sounds."	▸ "You're pausing every two words. Try to read up to the punctuation before taking a breath." ▸ "That's a *definition*. Try to use more of the information on the page to give an *explanation*."	▸ "Did you notice what you did there to figure out that tricky word?" ▸ "What kind of person is your character?"

Prompt types, purposes, and examples

Type of Prompt or Feedback	COMPLIMENT	SENTENCE STARTER
Purpose	To reinforce something the reader does that they should continue doing.	To nudge the reader by offering a bit of language.
Example	▸ "I noticed you didn't just sound the word out—you thought about what would make sense in this part." ▸ "I can tell you got information from the features and the text to come up with that main idea."	▸ "In the beginning . . ." ▸ "One fact is . . ."

ALIGNING STRATEGIES AND PROMPTS

When you offer students feedback during the coaching phase of a conference, make sure you use prompting language that is aligned to, or even borrowed from, the language of the strategy you're teaching. Your aim is to prompt the reader to do the work outlined in the strategy. Prompts that *do not align*, although possibly connected to the same goal, prompt the reader to use a different strategy, which can be confusing.

Strategy	Prompts That Align with the Strategy	Prompts That Do *Not* Align with the Strategy
Goal: Vocabulary "When you come to an unfamiliar word, think about the 'job' the word has in a sentence. Is it a noun, verb, adjective, or adverb? Use your knowledge of the job of the word to help you figure out what the word might mean."	▶ "What job does that word have in this sentence?" ▶ "Think about what kind of word it comes after [or before]. Does that help you figure out the job it has?" ▶ "Is the word a noun, verb, adjective, or adverb?"	▶ "Use context clues." ▶ "Think about where you've seen that word before." ▶ "Let's check the glossary to see if we can figure it out."

Strategy	Prompts That Align with the Strategy	Prompts That Do *Not* Align with the Strategy
Goal: Themes and Ideas		
"Pause in a place where the character's feelings change. Notice what causes the character's feelings to change. Think, 'What did they learn in that moment of the story?'"	▸ "Find a place where the character's feelings change for better or for worse." ▸ "Reread that spot with the change in feelings." ▸ "What do you think the character learned?"	▸ "What book does this story remind you of?" Do you think the two stories have a similar lesson?? ▸ "Think about what lesson the secondary character offers the main character." ▸ "Use the problem in the story to figure out a lesson."

PROMPTS AND LEVELS OF SUPPORT

Many years ago, I was in a leadership group led by Carl Anderson at the Teachers College Reading and Writing Project. I was a classroom teacher at the time, and I looked forward to learning from the master of writing conferences. Carl asked us to record our conferences (at that time, with a tape recorder) and then type a transcript (this was before the days of Dragon Dictation software or online transcription services). I remember sitting at the bright orange triangular Mac computer in my classroom after the kids had gone home, hitting *play* then *pause* then *play* then *pause*, typing up what my student and I had said. Then each Tuesday afternoon we'd bring our transcripts and critique each other and ourselves.

This study taught me so much about my sometimes-tendency to do too much of the work and too much of the talking, the patterns in the ways I offered students feedback, and what sorts of prompts yielded what sorts of responses. I used to begin every conference with a short demonstration of the strategy, and then I'd jump right in with the highest levels of help and support.

Over time, I've learned that I can often skip a demonstration. I also learned to start with as little support as possible in the coaching and prompting that happens after I offer students the steps of a strategy. "Go ahead and give it a try," I say, and then I try to back off and see what they can do. They know I am there for help if they need it.

As you confer, consider starting with prompts offering less support, like those in the bottom half of the chart on page 67. Notice that the prompts are brief and are often directives. If students struggle a bit with the strategy, allow wait time, and then, if they still need more help, jump in with a prompt that offers more support, such as one from the top row. Sometimes, though, I find that if I offer a small amount of support, I don't need to offer any more: the student just takes off. In this case, I will typically offer some positive feedback in the form of a compliment prompt (e.g., "Based on your description I can really picture it, too!").

Strategy

Try to experience all the author is describing by using all your senses. Read a little, then pause. Think, "What do I see? Hear? Feel? Taste? Smell?"

Prompts Offering More Support

▸ "What do you see? Hear? Taste? Smell?"

▸ "That's what the text says. What are you picturing?"

▸ "If you close your eyes, can you imagine the place? Tell me in detail what you're seeing. We'll start with that sense and go on from there."

Prompts Offering Less Support

▸ [Nonverbal: gesture to nose, mouth, and eyes to prompt for different senses.]

▸ "Stop here. Use your senses."

▸ "Describe it."

Varying levels of support with prompting

RESEARCH-COMPLIMENT-TEACH CONFERENCES

Structure and Timing

Lucy Calkins introduced me to this type of conference in *The Art of Teaching Writing* (1994). In Research-Compliment-Teach (RCD) Conferences, the teacher takes a minute or so to research (assess) before deciding what to teach. Eight out of ten times, this is the type of conference I'm using. I find that spending a moment or two to find out how a student's reading has been going has a number of benefits.

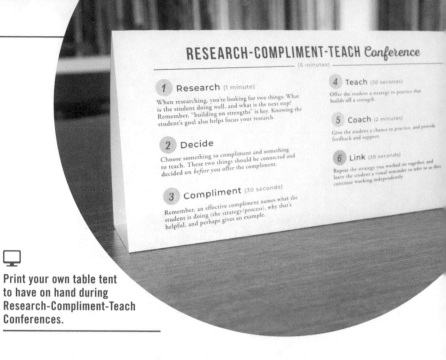

Print your own table tent to have on hand during Research-Compliment-Teach Conferences.

It holds students accountable. When I start with "Last time we worked on . . . Show me how that's been going," I am sending the message that I expect students use a strategy in between our meetings.

It gives students a chance to advocate for what they need. Instead of just beginning with whatever I think they need, students have a chance to reflect on their work, voice what's gone well, and ask for help with what's been tricky.

It helps me get oriented. Often, several days pass between conferences, and a lot can happen in that time. A student may suddenly be independent with a strategy I thought she needed more help with, a student may have read a book (or two or three) between the last meeting and this one, or there may be some new student work (reading responses, sticky notes, and so on) that I haven't yet had a chance to see.

The Research-Compliment-Teach Conference lasts about five minutes and follows a predictable structure:

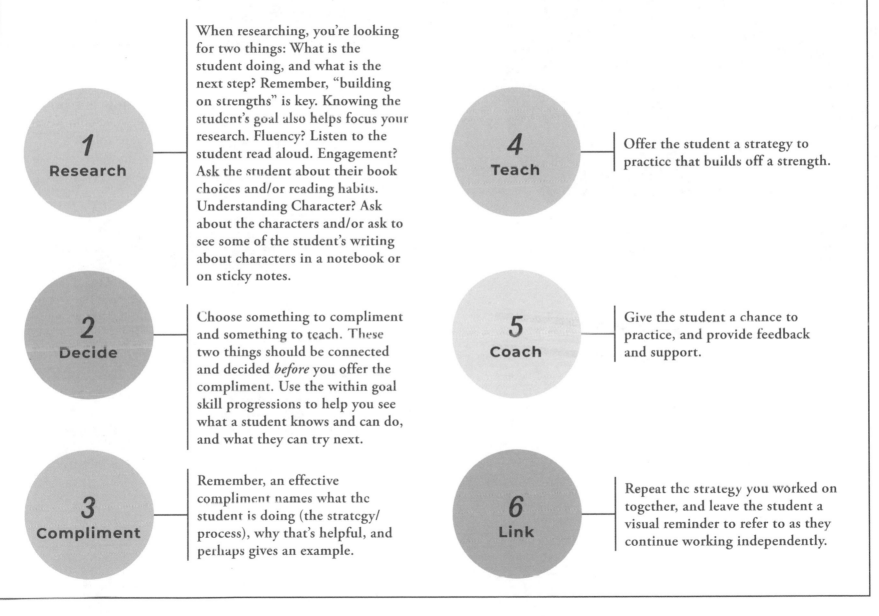

1 Research

When researching, you're looking for two things: What is the student doing, and what is the next step? Remember, "building on strengths" is key. Knowing the student's goal also helps focus your research. Fluency? Listen to the student read aloud. Engagement? Ask the student about their book choices and/or reading habits. Understanding Character? Ask about the characters and/or ask to see some of the student's writing about characters in a notebook or on sticky notes.

2 Decide

Choose something to compliment and something to teach. These two things should be connected and decided *before* you offer the compliment. Use the within goal skill progressions to help you see what a student knows and can do, and what they can try next.

3 Compliment

Remember, an effective compliment names what the student is doing (the strategy/process), why that's helpful, and perhaps gives an example.

4 Teach

Offer the student a strategy to practice that builds off a strength.

5 Coach

Give the student a chance to practice, and provide feedback and support.

6 Link

Repeat the strategy you worked on together, and leave the student a visual reminder to refer to as they continue working independently.

Watch a conference with Lucas, a second grader who is working on a goal of understanding Vocabulary. You can also read an annotated transcript.

Get a close-up look at my notes from this conference in the online resources. There you can also find blank conferring forms for each goal, complete with skill progressions and sample research questions, to offer you support as you confer with your readers.

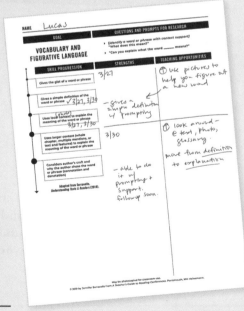

WATCH AND READ
A Research-Compliment-Teach Conference Example

As I research, I think about how students tend to progress with a goal. Lucas is working on a goal of understanding Vocabulary, so as I research I keep the following skill progression in mind:

Gives the gist of a word or phrase

Gives a simple definition of the word or phrase

Uses local context to explain the meaning of the word or phrase

Uses larger context (whole chapter, multiple mentions, or text and features) to explain the meaning of the word or phrase)

Considers author's craft and why the author chose the word or phrase (connotation and denotation)

Here are some teaching moves to notice as you watch:

▶ I start off by reminding Lucas of his last conference with me ("When we last spoke . . .") and immediately assess his work *within* his goal.

▶ I offer him a compliment and segue to a new strategy with the word *and*. This communicates that what I'm teaching today is a natural outgrowth of what he can already do.

▶ I give a quick demonstration. I don't always do this, but I choose to when I think the student might need extra support. When I demonstrate, notice how I voice-over my thinking. This way, the result doesn't seem like magic. I'm showing my process, not just the end product.

▶ I quickly turn the work over to Lucas and spend most of the conference giving him a chance to practice with my support.

▶ I prompt him by reiterating steps of the strategy. I'm careful to *only* prompt for the strategy, even though other "teachable moments" may arise.

▶ I avoid talking about the *content* of the book; the prompts are general so that they will apply to any book Lucas chooses to read.

▶ Before sending him off, I repeat the steps of the strategy and give him a reason for why and when he'll want to use it.

When researching, you're looking for two things: What is the student doing, and what is the next step?

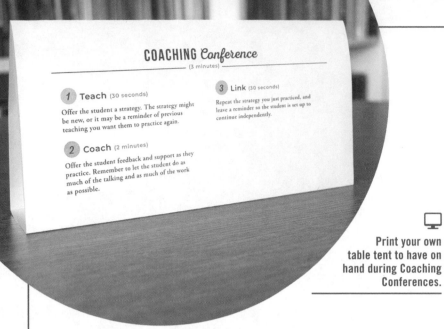

Print your own table tent to have on hand during Coaching Conferences.

COACHING CONFERENCES
Structure and Timing

Coaching Conferences cut to the chase, eliminating the research and compliment phases of the Research-Compliment-Teach Conference. When you are sure what you want to teach a student, Coaching Conferences help you save time. Perhaps you saw a student the day before, taught a new strategy, and noticed the student could use more support? You might choose to do a Coaching Conference the next day. Perhaps you just listened to students discussing a book in their book club, and you saw the conversation stalled because the topics they chose to discuss were too literal? You might meet with each student in a Coaching Conference to set them up to think about the text more deeply before their next book club conversation. Coaching Conferences usually last about three minutes, and, as the name would suggest, most of the time is spent . . . coaching!

1
Teach

Offer the student a strategy. The strategy might be new, or it may be a reminder of previous teaching you want them to practice again.

2
Coach

Offer the student feedback and support as they practice. Remember to let the student do as much of the talking and as much of the work as possible.

3
Link

Repeat the strategy you just practiced, and leave a reminder so the student is set up to continue independently.

WATCH AND READ
A Coaching Conference Example

Here are a few teaching moves to notice:

▸ I already know what I want to teach Ana, so I start right away by giving her the strategy. Twenty-five seconds into the conference, she's practicing.

▸ I notice that she tends to check with *me*, but I want her to check *herself*. So I use question prompts to get her to reflect on what she's doing as a reader to develop more self-awareness. ("Did that make sense?" "How do you know?")

▸ I frequently point out what Ana is doing well, alongside prompts to redirect her to try the strategy.

▸ I start with a lower level of support ("Can I hear you try it?"), work up to a higher level of support ("*Roll* would make sense. It has to be something else, though, because it doesn't end like *roll* would end. So what else looks right?"), and eventually end up with the highest level of support ("Could this word be *ride*?"). I want to make sure the student is doing the work, so I don't start with the most support right away.

Watch a Coaching Conference with Ana, a kindergartner who's working on a Print Work goal. Read an annotated transcript online.

Get a close-up look at my notes from this conference in the online resources, where you can also find blank conferring forms for each goal, complete with skill progressions and sample research questions, to offer you support as you confer with your readers.

STRATEGY LESSONS
Structure and Timing

Once you have the hang of providing meaningful, strategy-focused, in-the-moment feedback in one-on-one Coaching Conferences, you can group two or three students who are working on the same goal and who would benefit from the same strategy (Calkins 2000; Serravallo 2010). In a Strategy Lesson, you set a small group of students up to work on a strategy, just like with a Coaching Conference. But now, instead of coaching only one student, you will keep *all* the students in the group working independently while you coach them *individually*. This helps you work efficiently.

Strategy Lessons are *not* the same thing as Guided Reading. They are different in terms of length, material, purpose, and structure:

Strategy Lessons

Each reader brings a self-selected text.

Readers practice on an independent-level text.

The lesson is focused on one strategy.

All coaching is focused on one strategy but responds to individual needs within that strategy.

The lesson takes 5–10 minutes.

Strategies for any goal—from Engagement to Print Work to Writing About Reading—can be taught.

The teacher introduces a strategy.

Why? To support student goals within *independent*-level texts.

For students reading books at levels A–Z.

The lesson takes place in a small group.

Students are taught reading skills and strategies.

Guided practice occurs.

Guided Reading

The teacher selects the text and all in the group read the same one.

Readers practice on an instructional-level text.

The lesson is focused on skills readers need to be successful in reading texts at their instructional level.

Coaching can respond to students' needs and may be different for each student.

The lesson takes 20+ minutes.

Lessons focus mostly on Print Work, Fluency, and/or Comprehension.

The teacher introduces the text (and possibly also a strategy).

Why? To support students as they work with *instructional*-level texts.

For students reading books at levels A–J.

The Strategy Lesson structure is the same as that of a Coaching Conference. In *Teaching Reading in Small Groups* (2010), I liken the teacher's role to that of a plate spinner. At the beginning, you aim to get all the plates spinning (all the kids working). Then, you'll find a plate wobbles (the student needs an extra boost of coaching to keep going). Just as you get that plate back up and spinning (the student resumes practicing the strategy independently), another plate starts to teeter. The coaching pattern, therefore, feels swift: I spend about thirty seconds with one student before moving on to another, and then another, and then another, and then maybe back around offering one more bit of feedback to each student before sending them off to work independently.

Strategy Lessons go like this:

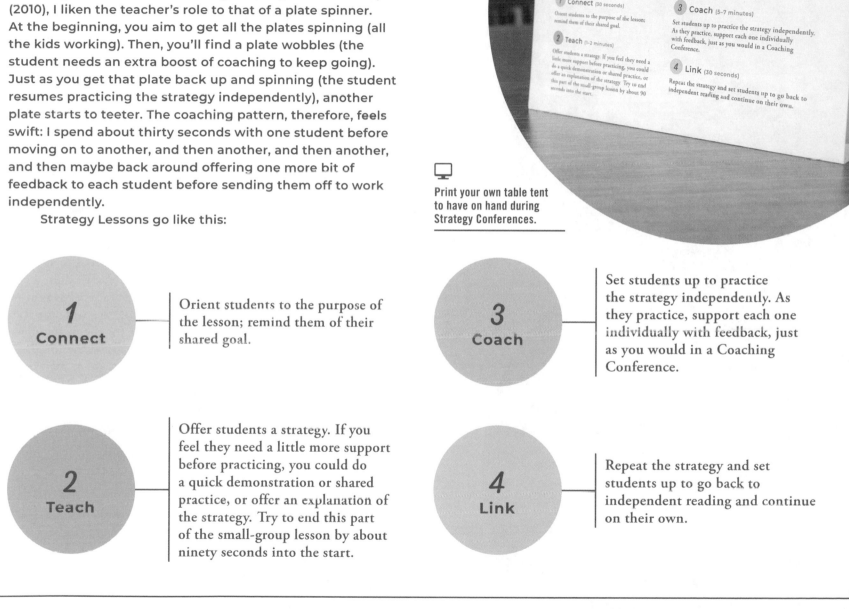

Print your own table tent to have on hand during Strategy Conferences.

1 Connect — Orient students to the purpose of the lesson; remind them of their shared goal.

2 Teach — Offer students a strategy. If you feel they need a little more support before practicing, you could do a quick demonstration or shared practice, or offer an explanation of the strategy. Try to end this part of the small-group lesson by about ninety seconds into the start.

3 Coach — Set students up to practice the strategy independently. As they practice, support each one individually with feedback, just as you would in a Coaching Conference.

4 Link — Repeat the strategy and set students up to go back to independent reading and continue on their own.

Watch a Strategy Lesson with a group of kindergarten readers who are practicing inferring character feelings . . .

. . . and/or a group of eighth graders who are considering how the mood of a setting affects characters. You can also read annotated transcripts of both lessons.

WATCH AND READ
Strategy Lesson Examples

Here are some important teaching moves to notice in the strategy lessons:

▸ I keep my lesson setup brief. With the kindergartners, in addition to introducing the strategy, I review some vocabulary for describing character feelings that I know they need based on prior teaching. With the eighth graders, I simply tell them the strategy and get them started.

▸ Because each student is practicing in their own chosen book, they are engaged and they practice the strategy in the book they will continue reading (or rereading in the case of kindergarteners). The kindergartners chose their books from a stack I'd selected to support the strategy they'd be practicing (books at levels C and D don't always have clear character emotion). The eighth graders brought along their independent reading books (all fiction, so I was sure the strategy would work). Given the strategy I chose for them, this also helps them get to the practice quickly, since they are in the middle of their books rather than on page 1.

▸ I coach each student based on their individual needs. The strategy is the same, but each reader might need a different type of coaching, a different level of support, or a slight tweak on the strategy.

▸ While I'm coaching, the other students are continuing to read and think independently, not waiting for me to come to them.

▶ Because I spend a short amount of time with each student, I'm able to circle back and check in with each again if I want. This way, they have repeated practice and feedback, trying the strategy in more than one spot in their books.

▶ I end the lesson by reminding students of what we practiced, articulating expectations that they'll continue to practice during their independent reading time.

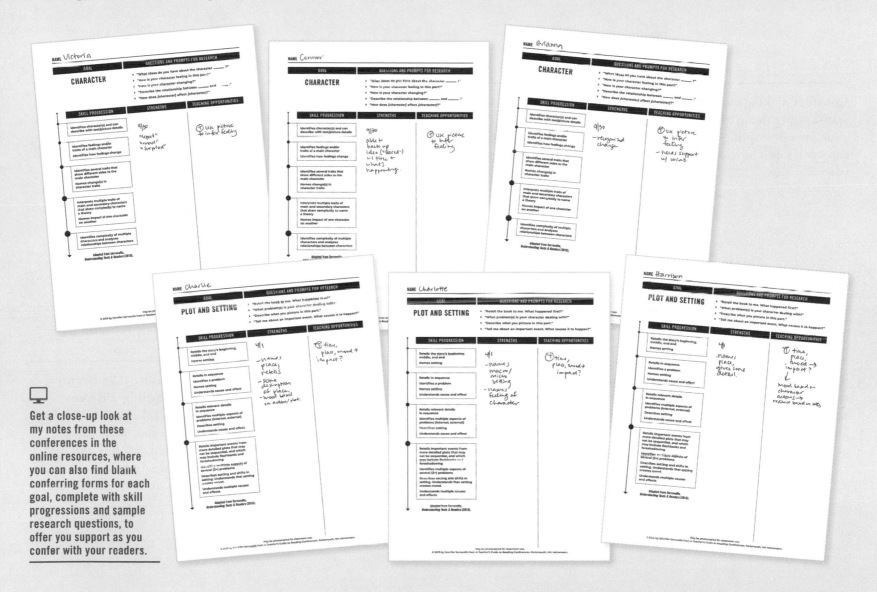

Get a close-up look at my notes from these conferences in the online resources, where you can also find blank conferring forms for each goal, complete with skill progressions and sample research questions, to offer you support as you confer with your readers.

{ *Take It to*
YOUR CLASSROOM

Here are some tips to help you bring Research-Compliment-Teach Conferences, Coaching Conferences, and Strategy Lessons to your classroom:

Consider making video or audio records of your conferences, transcribing them, and then spending some time reflecting on your own prompting patterns. It's incredible to see what you can notice and how your reflections can transform your teaching.

Some teachers find Coaching Conferences "easier" because they are, in essence, planned. You might focus just on this conference type for a week, using recent assessments, observations of students, or quick check-ins to gather the information you need to plan. If you have *The Reading Strategies Book* (Serravallo 2015), you can even flag individual strategy pages with student names and carry the book with you as you confer. When you get the hang of Coaching Conferences, try a Strategy Lesson with two students. Then, when you're ready, work your way up to a group of three.

Remember to make Research-Compliment-Teach Conferences more doable by focusing your research on the student's goal and keeping in mind the skill progressions within each goal. Download the note-taking forms with progressions and sample questions to keep with you as you confer. 🖥

Don't forget to take notes! With a class of more than twenty students, each with their own goals, each reading different books, you can't trust your memory with all the details. Record what you complimented, what you taught, and notes on how the student responded. These notes can help you link the next conference to the last one ("Last time we worked on . . ."), and sometimes you'll notice trends in the class so that you can pull meaningful small groups.

Mentor Spotlight
LUCY CALKINS

Lucy Calkins is the founder and leader of the Reading and Writing Project at Teachers College, Columbia University, where many literacy authors (including me!) went from being classroom teachers to staff developers and authors. I credit much of my knowledge and success in education to Lucy's visionary leadership and unwavering high expectations for everyone who had the good fortune to work at her organization. She is the prolific author of countless professional books and curricular resources about the teaching of

reading and writing. At a recent NCTE conference, I watched videos of Lucy masterfully conferring with young writers when she was a graduate student in what must have been the early 1980s. Her deep respect for children, and her awe of how they think and learn, came through in these videos, as it still does in her work today. I recommend getting to Teachers College to hear her speak, and reading her work firsthand. She graciously agreed to lend her voice by answering a few questions about conferring.

My advice: Start your reading here

JEN: Watching you confer with young children is nothing short of magic. What advice can you give about a teacher's tone during a conference?

LUCY CALKINS: We all have people in our lives who listen to us with such a keenness and intensity, listening to the words and the spaces between the words, that we end up saying more than we knew we had to say. When conferring, try to listen to the child as those people have listened to you. Be present with the child. Guard against pretending to listen while your eyes roam the room and your mind races ahead of you. Be present. Be there for the child.

Then, too, remember that in a good conference, the writer's energy for reading and writing goes up, not down. The child leaves you wanting to return to work. Keep an eye on the child's energy and teach in ways that ignite that energy. You'll find that children want concrete specific tips and they want to learn, as long as they sense that you see potential in them.

JEN: One of your greatest influences is Don Graves. What is one tip he taught you (either explicitly or through his modeling) about conferring that you carry with you?

LUCY CALKINS: I remember my first day as a researcher with Don Graves on a big federal study of children as writers. I had been a classroom teacher when Don asked me to leave the classroom and join him. We went into a classroom together. I had my clipboard and was ready to take notes on the kids as they wrote. But nobody was writing; they were just copying math problems out of a textbook. I roamed the aisles for a bit, waiting for some data to appear, and then, frustrated, I went back and sat on the radiator waiting for the kids to do something I could record. Meanwhile, Graves had been scurrying around the classroom, head down, writing. Finally, tired of waiting, I signaled him, saying, "Don, let's go." We went out into the hall. Before I could let out a groan, Don turned to me and said, "Zowee! Wasn't that amazing?"

I said, "Yeah? What'd you see?" And he launched into a detailed account of all he'd seen and wondered and marveled at. "Kids with chairs so low and desks so high," and then he mimicked how they were writing on desks, shoulder high. "And that one kid with an eraser the size of golf ball, and that little kid with the pencil the size of a tiny stub. How could they write?"

I learned something that day, and I think it was one of the greatest lessons that Don taught me. I learned to see significance in the detail, in the grit of life. That matters. As teachers, we see the smallest things: a child balls up the page and throws it on the floor. We're fascinated. We retrieve the discarded page and smooth it out. We ask the child, "What didn't you like about your draft?" and we probe, "If you *were* going to make it better, what would you do?" Those questions lead to theories, and to newly attentive continued watching.

That's teaching. That's writing. That's a big part of what Don taught me.

He would find pleasure and insight in the ordinary, almost mundane details of life. He'd watch a teacher going through her mail, putting stuff in the garbage, and the next day he'd give a keynote, turning that moment into a metaphor as he talked about all the garbage that we have to wade through as teachers.

When I see meaning and beauty in the details of life, I'm drawing on life lessons that Graves taught me.

JEN: How would you advise teachers to build a knowledge base for conferring in reading?

LUCY CALKINS: It's easy to feel empty-handed when you pull a chair alongside a child who is reading a book that you don't know. I find it helps to remember all the sources of meaning you can draw upon in those moments.

First, you draw on your own experience as a reader. You note the work the text requires a reader to do, and you watch and notice what the child is doing in response to the challenges the text poses. You think about what you, as a more proficient reader, would do. For example, if you note that time in the story seems to be jumping around and you find that when you read the text, you need to pause from time to time to ask, "Wait, when is this? Where is this?" then you wonder whether the child is doing that sort of work. You may notice a space between what the child's doing and what you'd do as a reader. You think, "Am I doing something that I can help the child to participate in as well, or that I can reveal to the child?" That's one source for your teaching.

Then, too, even if you do not know the book the child is reading, you know the genre, and your knowledge of the genre becomes a resource you draw on as you teach. If this is a mystery, you can ask the child whether he is collecting clues. If this is historical fiction, you can ask whether trouble is brewing in the world of the story and press the reader to consider how various characters are responding differently to that trouble.

There are a number of other resources you can draw upon to help you have content to teach in a reading conference. For example, presumably you have been teaching the class some important skills. Perhaps you've been teaching readers to develop theories about characters. You can listen to the child's thinking and look at any writing she has done about the text, thinking, "Of all that I have taught the child to do, what is the child initiating on her own? What might make this work even better?"

There are many other sources that you can draw upon when conferring about a book that you don't know well. The important thing is to remember that you are teaching the reader, not the book.

JEN: What do you think might make reading conferring easier?

LUCY CALKINS: I think it is easier to confer with readers if you have a sense of how reading skills develop over time. If you know what prediction looks like for very young readers, and you know what it looks like as those readers become older and more skilled, and what it looks like for a strong middle school reader, for example, then you can draw on your knowledge of that trajectory when you confer. You watch and listen to the child, thinking, "Where is this child on the trajectory? What's the next important step the child could take?"

For example, if the child is predicting by thinking mostly about what will happen at the end of the book, I might think, "All right. The child is paying attention to the plot and

thinking in big sweeping steps. What's next for her?" Maybe I'd teach that child to predict not only *what* will happen next, but also *how* it will happen. I might also coach her to draw on what she knows about the protagonist in order to hypothesize how things will unfold in the text.

It is helpful to remember that if we teach something that is five steps beyond the work that reader is currently doing, it's unlikely that the child will be able to continue to do that work without us. Always, the goal is to nudge and support the reader into doing work that's just bit of a stretch. We need to be able to pull back and let the child do that work on his or her own.

JEN: What do you think makes reading conferring hard for some teachers?

LUCY CALKINS: Conferring is like coaching in a basketball game. You can't really coach unless the players can carry on playing the game. The players have to know how to go up and down the court, making baskets. The players need to know the gist of the game in order for us to be able to coach.

My point is that coaching is important, but it isn't everything. You also need to teach the whole class in such a way that they know how to carry on with some independence. Only then can you confer, can you coach.

Then, too, you'll listen to and watch your kids as they work, and you'll use your observations to plan your teaching. Some of that teaching will occur through your one-to-one coaching, but other parts of that teaching will happen as you read aloud, lead small groups, teach minilessons, and support shared reading. Conferring is just one piece of it all.

My other bit of advice is this: stop beating yourself up. You won't reach every child every week in your conferences, and that has to be okay. After a good conference, go back to that child a day or two later to see the results. You need that feedback on your teaching, that way to hold yourself accountable for actually lifting the level of what your students do when they aren't with you. Your conferences constitute the course you give yourself so that you learn from your teaching. Aim to be surprised by your children, perplexed by them, and changed by them. Expect your conferences to help you become a more responsive teacher. You need your conferring to be a source of insight, a way for you to be in touch with your kids, and a way to hold yourself accountable for the kind of teaching that yields results. When your conferring doesn't work, try something new.

Conferring is the epitome of teaching. It's the hardest thing you do, because you never step in the same river twice. But ultimately, when you're good at conferring, then that conferring becomes a computer chip that generates all the rest of your teaching.

chapter six

SUPPORTING CONVERSATION
and Collaboration

Book clubs and partnerships offer students an important chance to meet with peers, which makes reading more social. Partnerships and clubs can also bolster students' reading skills. Young children can increase their reading stamina when, after reading independently for a while, they have a chance to read with a friend. Students in these pairs can support each other's print and fluency strategies or practice strategies that require another person, like acting out scenes by pretending to be the characters. In conversations, students use valuable speaking and listening skills to deepen their understandings about texts, correct misunderstandings, and see new perspectives.

Partnerships and Clubs in the Classroom

As students move through the grades, the sorts of work they do in partnerships and clubs often changes.

Most kindergarten through second-grade teachers make time for kids to meet for five to ten minutes in ability-based partnerships every day either before or after independent reading. Partners come together, each with their own baggie of self-selected books, choose one book to put between them, and then either read the pages together at the same time (chorally) or take turns reading pages. As children read, they may stumble over a word or their fluency may sound choppy, at which point a partner can be taught to prompt their peer—just like a teacher would—to use a strategy. Partners can also compliment teach other ("That sounded smooth!") or cheer each other on ("Try it! I know you can figure that word out."). As they come to parts that are funny or surprising, or that they want to discuss, partners may pause reading to have a quick chat, or even to act out a part. Other students may save the conversation or dramatizing for the end of the book.

In grades three and above (and sometimes even second grade), students read mostly chapter books. Partners therefore meet to discuss what they've already read, rather than spend partner time doing the reading together. Students may choose a book to read at the same pace (as long as there are multiple copies of titles available so they can read simultaneously), or they may each finish a book independently and then swap and read their partner's book before discussing (i.e., Partner A reads one Cam Jansen mystery while Partner B reads another). Teachers often find that having partnerships meet to discuss their books a couple of times a week for a longer block of time (ten to fifteen minutes) works better than every day for a shorter period of time. When students meet too frequently, they often haven't read enough new pages in their books to warrant a meaty discussion.

After students have some experience with partnerships, teachers may choose to set them up in book clubs. Working with peers in a group of four to six, students decide together what book to read, read the book at the same pace (i.e., stopping on Chapter 4 by Wednesday and Chapter 8 by Friday), and meet a couple of times a week to discuss the book. For book clubs, multiple copies of books are necessary. If you are low on resources, you might try starting book clubs with reproducible short texts such as short stories or nonfiction articles.

Spotlight on
EMERGENT BILINGUALS

Leveraging Talk Time

▸ Students need access to proficient language models for input, and opportunity to practice their language through speaking (Gibbons 2015). Book clubs and reading partnerships can offer both.

▸ In individual conferences, you might prepare students for conversations with peers by practicing new language structures, getting comfortable with vocabulary, or even practicing what they might say.

▸ Be sure to group students with others who are strong language models.

▸ Providing students with language frames and sentence starters before and during conversations can help them use new language structures.

▸ Some students may be most comfortable speaking in their home language, or a combination of their home language and second language, as they discuss ideas from their book.

PARTNERSHIP CONFERENCES WITH YOUNG READERS
Structure and Timing

With kindergarten and early-first-grade readers, I often teach skills for being productive in a partnership (sitting hip to hip, putting one book between you, deciding who gets to pick the book, alternate-page reading or choral reading, etc.), or I work with children on the same foundational skills they are working on during independent reading (i.e., Print Work strategies or Fluency strategies). Once students are functioning independently and productively in the partnership and their reading improves in accuracy and fluency, then I move on to comprehension and conversation strategies.

Partnership Conferences with young readers are often short—around three minutes—and follow a structure that is very similar to individual Research-Compliment-Teach Conferences with one important difference: your role in the *research* phase is as a note-taker and listener; don't interrupt the partnership or ask questions.

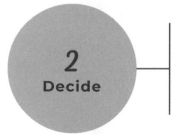

1 Research

Observe, listen, and take notes as students read and/or work together. Sit close enough to the book club or partnership so you can hear students clearly and take notes. Don't interrupt. If students start talking to you instead of their peers, redirect them with a nonverbal cue to put their eyes and ears back on their friends. You need to see what they can do without your support—if you start directing the conversation during your assessment, you'll get a skewed sense of their independent abilities. Think about what strengths they are exhibiting in terms of their partnership behaviors and reading skills.

2 Decide

Choose something to compliment and something to teach. As with individual conferences, try to make sure that the strategy you teach builds off the compliment.

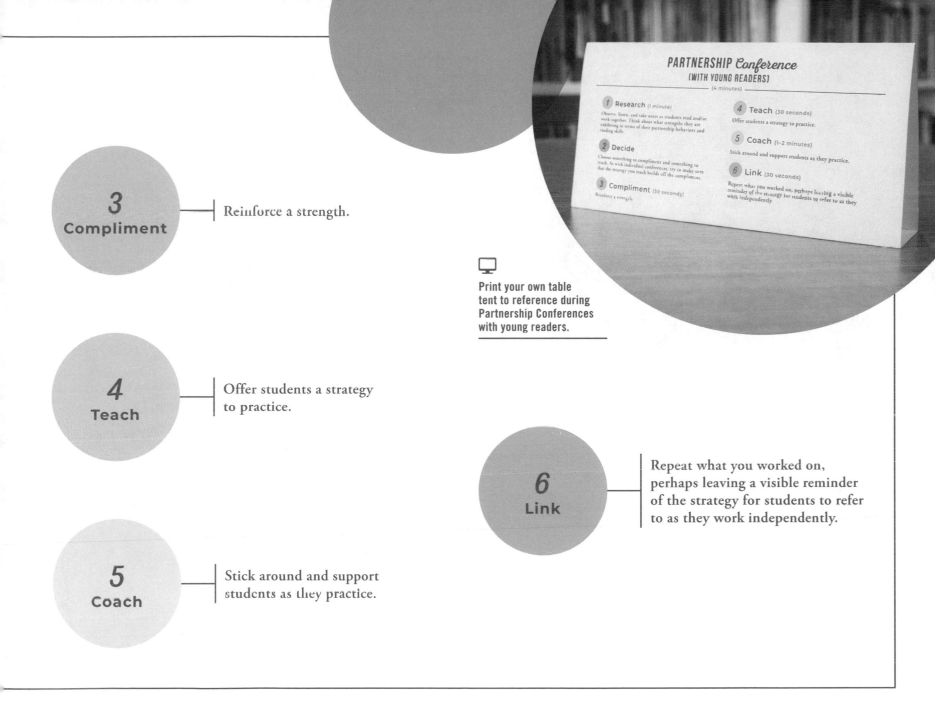

3
Compliment

Reinforce a strength.

4
Teach

Offer students a strategy to practice.

5
Coach

Stick around and support students as they practice.

6
Link

Repeat what you worked on, perhaps leaving a visible reminder of the strategy for students to refer to as they work independently.

Print your own table tent to reference during Partnership Conferences with young readers.

PARTNERSHIP *Conference*
(WITH YOUNG READERS)
(4 minutes)

1 Research (1 minute)
Observe, listen, and take notes as students read and/or work together. Think about what strengths they are exhibiting in terms of their partnership behaviors and reading skills.

2 Decide
Choose something to compliment and something to teach. As with individual conferences, try to make sure that the strategy you teach builds off the compliment.

3 Compliment (30 seconds)
Reinforce a strength.

4 Teach (30 seconds)
Offer students a strategy to practice.

5 Coach (1-2 minutes)
Stick around and support students as they practice.

6 Link (30 seconds)
Repeat what you worked on, perhaps leaving a visible reminder of the strategy for students to refer to as they work independently.

Watch a conference with Gabbie and Ashley, a pair of kindergartners. You can also read my notes and an annotated transcript of the conference online.

WATCH AND READ
A Partnership Conference Example

As you watch, you might notice

▸ At the beginning of the conference, I observe them without interrupting, looking for strengths and opportunities for growth connected to their individual goals and also their work as a partnership.

▸ I coach by getting one student to talk to the other, rather than addressing them both. ("Did she get it? What can you tell her?") This supports students with the sorts of language they will need as they work together, without a teacher's support, in the future.

▸ I create a partnership "menu" at the end of the conference. Like the individual goal cards, this menu gives them a way to refer back to the work we practiced together as they work independently.

Partnership or club menus, like this one from a second-grade classroom, can serve to support partnership routines in addition to reminding students of strategies they've learned. Routines can be helpful as students work to develop independence and stamina. (From *The Reading Strategies Book* [Serravallo 2015].)

Partner Routine
1-Prepare for partner time with post-its in your book.
2-Retell what you've read so far-your partner will rate it!
3-Choose from your Reading Menu
4-Write a B♥B entry or add to one!

Act Out a Part That's:
-Dramatic
-Important
-Well-written
Then, talk back and forth

Talk About Confusing Parts:
-Was it a **tricky word?** Use all your strategies together!
-Did your **mental movie get blurry?** Reread it together and talk about it!

Share your Post-its or B♥B **entries!**
-Talk long back and forth about one idea
-Use the "Talking Map" to make a plan!

Simple partnership "menus" can help readers remember strategies to practice as they work together.

Gabbie + Ashley
PARTNER MENU
- - - - - - - - -

s-m-o-o-t-h

Teaching Talk (Speaking and Listening)

In partnerships and clubs, I may support readers with strategies connected to their independent goals (i.e., understanding Character, determining Main Idea, inferring the meaning of Vocabulary or Figurative Language, etc.), especially if their thinking about the text is literal or basic. Focusing on supporting deeper thinking about texts can get more conversation-worthy topics going. Other times, I may choose to support talk skills, especially if students are still working on listening to each other or sticking to a topic at all. Here's a progression of talk skills that I have in mind as I watch student discussions. Download a copy of this and other skill progressions from the online resources. 🖥

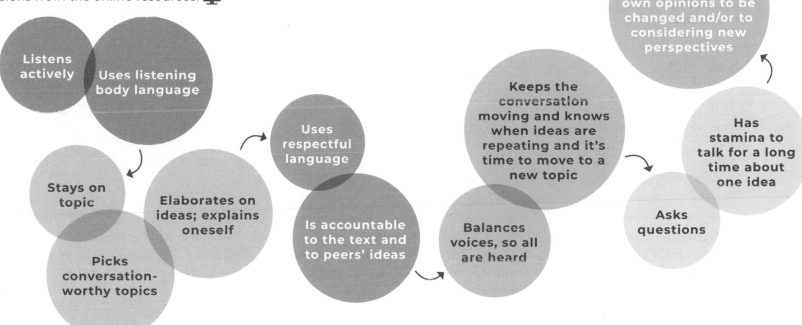

Progression of Conversation skills

PARTNERSHIPS AND BOOK CLUB CONFERENCES FOR CONVERSATION

Structure and Timing

Whether students are meeting to discuss books in partnerships or clubs, conferences to support them follow pretty much the same structure as the Partnership Conferences to support younger readers you read about earlier in the chapter. The entire conference will last about three to five minutes.

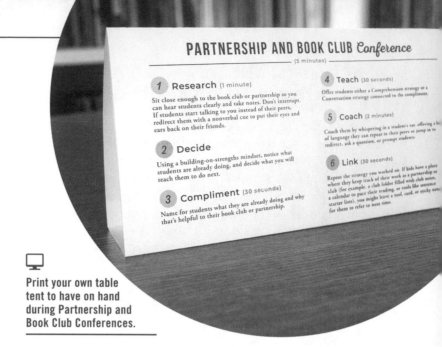

🖥 Print your own table tent to have on hand during Partnership and Book Club Conferences.

1
Research

Listen to the conversation, thinking about comprehension skills and conversation skills. Consider whether a strategy to deepen their conversation, or one focused more on speaking and listening, will help them most.

2
Decide

Using a building-on-strengths mindset, notice what students are already doing, and decide what you will teach them to do next.

3
Compliment

Name for students what they are already doing and why that's helpful to their book club or partnership.

4 Teach

Offer students either a comprehension strategy or a conversation strategy connected to the compliment.

5 Coach

Stick around as students practice. Sometimes you might coach them by whispering in a student's ear, offering a bit of language they can repeat to their peers. This helps them feel empowered to use that language again. Other times you might jump in to redirect, ask a question, or prompt students.

6 Link

Repeat the strategy you worked on. If kids have a place where they keep track of their work as a partnership or club (for example, a club folder filled with club notes, a calendar to pace their reading, or tools like sentence starter lists), you might leave a tool, card, or sticky note for them to refer to next time.

Your role in the research phase is as a note-taker and listener; don't interrupt the partnership or ask questions.

Watch a conference with a fourth-grade book club or read the annotated transcript of the conference.

Get a close-up look at my notes from this conference in the online resources, where you can also find blank conferring forms for each goal, complete with skill progressions and sample research questions, to offer you support as you confer with your readers.

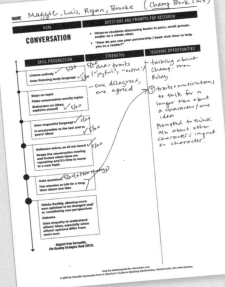

WATCH AND READ
A Book Club Conference Example

As you watch, you might notice

▶ For the first minute or two, I listen carefully and takes notes about both conversation skills and comprehension skills.

▶ Once I interrupt the conversation, I give students some positive feedback about conversational moves they are using that will help them in any conversation.

▶ I offer a strategy that builds off a strength—they could already take turns about one idea, and now I'm asking them to deepen their thinking as they take turns. I state the new work as a step-by-step strategy.

▶ As they practice, I stick around to listen and take notes. I coach when needed, to support their practice.

▶ Sometimes my coaching involves stopping the whole group to prompt them all to think or try something ("Are there any other characters who are having an impact on Riley?"). Another time, I whisper into the ear of one of the students to give her language to use with the whole group ("Do you know why . . . ?"). I find whenever I can get the students to use new language, it becomes more likely they will use it again independently soon.

▶ When students look to me for approval, I redirect them back to each other. I try to stay on the sidelines, encouraging their independence as they keep the conversation moving.

Here are some tips for getting partnerships and clubs up and running successfully in your classroom—giving you valuable time to confer with small groups.

Students who have never been in partnerships or clubs may struggle to sustain collaborative work and/or conversation independently. You can scaffold their practice during the whole-class read-aloud. After reading a text, have students sit in a large circle and help them have a whole-class conversation. Try to stay outside the circle, jumping in only when needed. Encourage kids to call on each other or, better yet, to notice when there's quiet and chime in without the need of hand raising. Support their conversation and comprehension skills, and explain that what they are practicing during this whole-class time is the same work they need to practice when they are in smaller groupings. See Pranikoff (2017) or Peterson and Eeds (1990) for more information on whole-class conversations.

You might also coach students in "read-aloud clubs," small groups of four to six students who meet to discuss just as they do in an independent book club. However, for read-aloud clubs, you'll read the text to the students, scaffolding their comprehension along the way, so they will be better primed with things to say. Confer during read-aloud clubs just as you would during book clubs. For more on read-aloud clubs, see *Teaching Reading in Small Groups* (Serravallo 2010).

You could choose to have all kids meet in partnerships and clubs at the same time and on the same days and float around and confer, or you could schedule each club to meet on a different day and plan to be there as they practice.

Mentor Spotlight
ELLIN KEENE

When I was a new teacher, a mentor of mine looked me in the eyes, handed me a copy of Ellin Keene and Susan Zimmermann's first edition of *Mosaic of Thought* (1997), and said, "You *must* read this." She wasn't wrong. And today, rarely a week goes by without my giving the same advice to someone else. In that book, and in her other books about comprehension and conversation, Ellin demystifies comprehension by showing and telling what it can look like. She graciously agreed to answer a few questions about the ways in which conversation can support comprehension.

My advice: Start your reading here

JEN: How does student discussion about books support comprehension?

ELLIN KEENE: I sometimes wonder if we are truly comprehending if we *aren't* involved in conversation about texts. Talk gives shape and substance to readers' evolving understanding of texts. Multiple perspectives on text inform, persuade, and help readers shift their perspectives. Other voices help us broaden our worldview and engage us, ensuring that we'll remember and reapply the ideas that spring from texts well after we've read the book.

JEN: I love your latest book, *Engaging Children* (2018). What is the difference between students *participating* in conversation and students *engaged* in conversation?

ELLIN KEENE: Mere participation can feel rote and rigid sometimes. I've observed book clubs and conversations about books where students' central concern seems to be to say something—anything—because they've been told to do so. Engagement happens when kids are literally leaning in to the conversation, so eager to share an insight that they may even talk over one another. Engagement often leads to some or all of the students actually changing their perspectives on the book, discovering new meaning as their peers speak. I love to see surprise on the faces of kids in a discussion, and a little edge, just a little friction (in a civil way, of course!), feeds engagement. If readers feel strongly enough to advocate for a position in a conversation, they're probably engaged. I must acknowledge, though, that the text has to be right. It has to have substance and be meaty enough for students to dig in for truly engaged conversation!

JEN: When kidwatching during a conversation, what signs show a teacher it's going well?

ELLIN KEENE: Leaning in (literally), looks of surprise and awe, quickening the pace of talk, and a little increase in volume are often signs of engaged conversation. However, it is very important, in my view, to look for the child who is leaning *back*, reflecting to develop his or her thoughts. Great conversation includes moments of silence and we teachers should encourage all members (those who are usually extroverted and those who tend to be introverted) to use silence to let thoughts develop. *Adults* tend to be less comfortable with silence and we inadvertently pass that feeling on to students. We need to model how to slow it down a bit and make way for thought.

JEN: What do you see as the teacher's role in supporting student discussion?

ELLIN KEENE: Frequently throughout the year, we need to model for students what stimulating conversation about text looks, sounds, and feels like. I would also suggest that we become very aware of our own tendency to interrupt, complete students' sentences, or in other ways "lead the witnesses" to say what we hope they will say! These ubiquitous practices not only rob children of the agency they need to take some risks in conversations, but also create the impression that we don't believe they're going to "get there." Given that there are so many possible interpretations in well-written texts, there really is no there there! Our role is to observe carefully, to listen with all our attentiveness, and to provide feedback following a conversation. In other words, and I'm often guilty of not doing this enough, we need to bite our tongues until they're Swiss cheese!

JEN: For teachers who have not yet made student discussions about literature a part of their classrooms, what would you say to give them courage to try it?

ELLIN KEENE: Try it with a colleague first! Be aware of what is stimulating and satisfying as you talk with colleagues and/or friends, and take cues from your own experiences—let them lead you to effective practices with children. There isn't a right or wrong way to set up student conversations. They just need to feel authentic. Start with an excerpt or shorter text that you and your students already love. Avoid the temptation to write out a bunch of questions that will stifle the conversation—after all, do you ask your friends comprehension questions in your book club? Start, perhaps, by asking the students what *they* wonder as they hear or read the text again (rereading is air and water to great book conversations), and then share their thinking. You'll be thrilled with the outcome—all kids have great thinking about books—they're just waiting for the opportunity to think out loud!

chapter seven

PLANNING AND MANAGING
Conferring Time

You've read about a variety of types of conferences to support your goal-directed instruction. Each type takes a slightly different amount of time, has a slightly different structure, and has a slightly different purpose.

At this point, your mind may be swimming with possibilities and you may be craving some organization for all you now know. Don't worry! I've got you covered. I'm the daughter of an analytical chemist and it's an understatement to say I've got a brain that thrives on organization and structure. First, turn the page to see a summary of all the different kinds of conferences we've considered across this book.

Conference Name	*chapter two* ASSESSMENT CONFERENCES	*chapter three* GOAL-SETTING CONFERENCES	*chapter four* COMPLIMENT CONFERENCES	*chapter five* COACHING CONFERENCES	*chapter five* RESEARCH-COMPLIMENT-TEACH CONFERENCES
Purposes	▸ Learn about the student. ▸ Involve the student in self-reflection. ▸ Figure out what area(s) of strength and what area(s) of need the student has. ▸ Make sure the student is matched well to their book(s).	▸ Involve the student in self-reflection. ▸ Establish a new goal.	▸ Reinforce strengths. ▸ Encourage a student's use of strategies. ▸ Monitor progress and check in.	▸ Teach a new strategy or reteach a previously taught strategy. ▸ Coach and give feedback. ▸ Save time when you know what you'll teach.	▸ Research what strategy would be most helpful to teach within a student's goal. ▸ Check in with the reader before deciding on today's strategy. ▸ Teach a new strategy or reteach a previously taught strategy. ▸ Offer the student time to practice with feedback from the teacher.
Timing	5–7 minutes	5 minutes	2 minutes	3 minutes	5 minutes

	Conference Name	
Conference Name	*chapter five* **STRATEGY LESSONS**	*chapter six* **PARTNERSHIP AND BOOK CLUB CONFERENCES**
Purposes	▸ Pull together two to four students who would benefit from the same strategy. ▸ Work efficiently by introducing the strategy to the whole group at once. ▸ Spend most of the time coaching students individually.	▸ Confer while students are engaged in reading together, acting out parts of their books, or are in conversation about a book. ▸ Take advantage of the ready-made small group of two to four students. ▸ Support students' individual goals, their collaboration, and/or their conversation.
Timing	7–10 minutes	4–5 minutes

That's a lot of conference possibilities, and before we move forward to consider how to manage them all in a busy classroom, I want to share a true story with you so you can learn from my mistakes.

When I was new to workshop teaching, I'd spend most of my planning time focused on whole-class lessons. Sometimes I'd even script out my lessons. I'd create a beautiful classroom chart. I was ready. Then I'd find myself ten minutes into my literacy block, minilesson over, having sent the kids back to their seats to read independently without any direction. For the next thirty to forty minutes I'd wander the classroom, conferring with students who caught my eye. Finally it occurred to me that I should *plan* for my conferring time. If I did, I could anticipate which students could be pulled together into groups, and I could be more efficient.

Instead of spending all my planning time on the first ten minutes, I began thinking about the students I would see that day and what they might need instead of always conferring off the cuff. The result? My conferences were shorter and more focused, and I was able to lead purposeful small groups, which saved time. This meant I doubled the number of children I was able to see each day.

Planning Your Conferring Time

When planning the schedule for your conferring time, here are my top five tips:

▶ When kids need the same strategy, see them in a group. But don't force kids into groups just because it's more convenient.

▶ Put groups on your plan first, conferences second.

▶ Try to get each student on your plan somehow (in a conference, in a small group, during book club time) at least twice a week.

▶ Leave yourself a little "buffer" time for makeups, conferences that run longer than anticipated, or time to sweep the room and give compliments.

▶ Be open to revising the plan as the week progresses! Kids get sick and are absent, a conference won't go as planned and you'll want a do-over, or you'll get some new information about a student that you want to respond to. Your weekly plan is your plan *for now*. It can change as the week goes by.

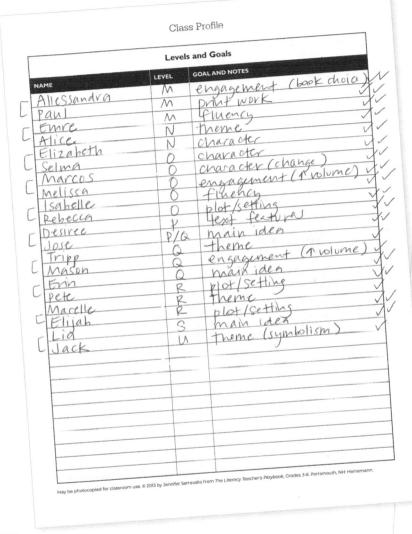

Class Profile

NAME	LEVEL	GOAL AND NOTES
Allessandra	M	engagement (book choice)
Paul	M	print work
Emre	M	fluency
Alice	N	theme
Elizabeth	N	character
Selma	O	character
Marcos	O	character (change)
Melissa	O	engagement (↑ volume)
Isabelle	O	fluency
Rebecca	O	plot/setting
Desiree	P	text feature
Jose	P/Q	main idea
Tripp	Q	theme
Mason	Q	engagement (↑ volume)
Erin	Q	main idea
Pete	R	plot/setting
Marelle	R	theme
Elijah	R	plot/setting
Lia	S	main idea
Jack	U	theme (symbolism)

May be photocopied for classroom use. © 2013 by Jennifer Serravallo from *The Literacy Teacher's Playbook, Grades 3–6.* Portsmouth, NH: Heinemann.

Here is a sample class list. Notice I've indicated the levels of books each student reads as well as their goal and other notes. This will help me notice patterns and group kids for strategy lessons. Find this blank form online.

Based on the class list, here is a weekly schedule. Notice I've left some time unscheduled to allow for makeups or to plan additional conferences for students who may need them. Find this blank form online.

Planning Your Week

	Monday	Tuesday	Wednesday	Thursday	Friday
Strategy Lesson (10 min)	Erin, Lia ⑦				Elijah + Pete ⑩
Strategy Lesson (10 min)	Melissa, Mason ⑦	Alice, Tripp, Marelle ⑩	Elijah, Pete, Rebecca ⑩	Jose, Erin, Lia ⑩	Elizabeth, Selma ⑦
Conferences (5 minutes each)	Allessandra ⑤ Isabelle ⑤	Jack ⑤ Desiree ⑤	Emre ⑤ Tripp ⑤	Paul ⑤ Mason ⑤ Jack ⑤	Marcos ⑤ Marelle ⑤
Guided Reading (15–20 min)					
Other (10 min) partner	Allessandra + Paul ⑤ Emre + Alice ⑤		Elizabeth + Selma ⑤ Marcos + Melissa ⑤		Isabelle + Rebecca ⑤ Desiree + Jose ⑤
Notes	*20 min flex	*10 min flex	*15 min flex		

May be photocopied for classroom use. © 2013 by Jennifer Serravallo from *The Literacy Teacher's Playbook, Grades 3–6.* Portsmouth, NH: Heinemann.

Which Conference Type Do I Choose?

Throughout the year, students will move through a continuing cycle of beginning a new goal, working on strategies for that goal and getting feedback as they practice, then moving on to new goals.

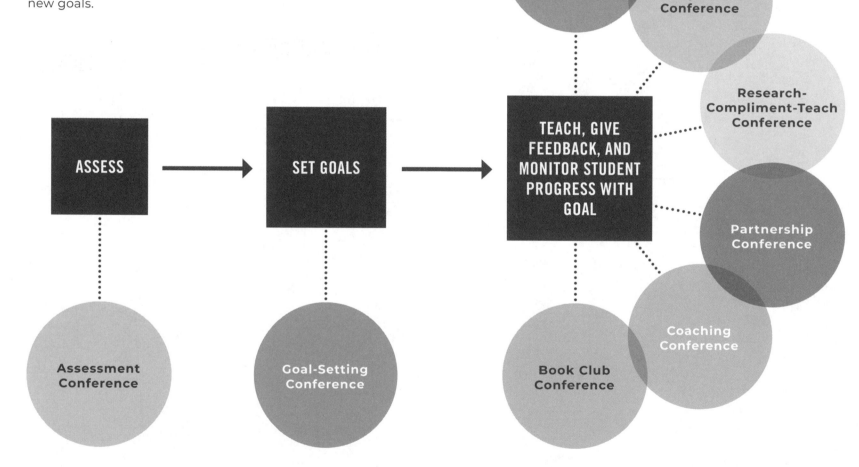

Students will also begin reading increasingly more challenging texts as the year progresses. As they read more challenging books, new challenges may arise for them as readers, warranting new goals.

There isn't a time of year when you'll be using any one conference type for all kids, though you will likely be doing a lot of Assessment and Goal-Setting Conferences in the first weeks of the school year. Instead, you'll be choosing your conference type to match your purpose and the kind of support a student needs. That will change week to week. Think, then, of the conference types as tools in a toolbox. Use a hammer to drive a nail, not a wrench. But when the handle on your sink needs tightening, remember that wrench. If you need extra time with a student to see how they are doing with their recently learned strategies, choose a Research-Compliment-Teach Conference. If you know there's a strategy a student needs to practice with support and feedback, choose a Coaching Conference. Not ready to teach something new and just want to reinforce a child's efforts? Choose a Compliment Conference.

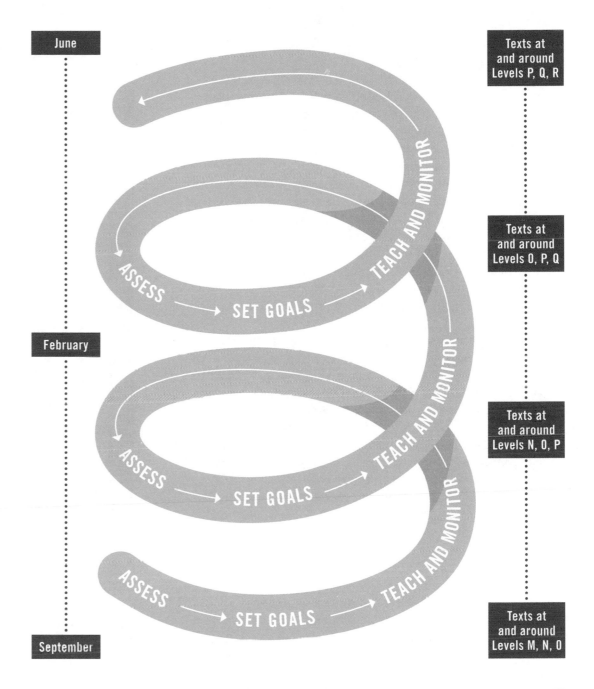

Balancing Individual Goals and Class Goals

At this point, you may be wondering how to balance what you're teaching during conferring with your whole-class curriculum and instruction. My inclination is to use conferring and small-group time *mostly* to support what individual students need and to offer strategies connected to their goals—not the goals from the unit of study or curriculum. I give students access to curriculum-based objectives during minilessons and read-alouds, time to practice during those lessons, and also some time for independent application. I will often send children off from whole-class lessons with advice to "use this today if _____ ," encouraging them to add the day's lesson to their repertoire, but knowing that any whole-class instruction is unlikely to be just right for every child on the same day.

If you find that students have a hard time knowing when to practice the whole-class lesson and when to practice the strategies connected to their individual goals, you might try segmenting the reading block with time set aside for each. Classroom charts that chronicle whole-class lessons, and individual goal cards that remind students of their individual goal and strategies, can be helpful visual tools to help students transition between the two chunks of time, and stay focused on separate goals during each time period.

Remember that the conference and small-group structures you've learned about are just that—structures. You can use these same structures in writing. In math. In art, PE, and music! So whether you decide to focus all your conferring time on supporting individual goals, or some time on class goals and some time on individual goals, conferring and small-group instruction offer students the guided practice they need to develop independence and automaticity with the strategies you teach.

	What?	Example
5–10 minutes	Whole-class minilesson (topic based on unit, curriculum, and/or standards)	Summarizing by rereading a text with a main idea in mind and finding key details that support the main idea
10 minutes	Conferring and small-group instruction based on whole-class goals	Small group of three students who need help with yesterday's lesson about finding main idea
30 minutes	Conferring and small-group instruction based on individual goals	Conference (Paul)—decoding strategy Small group (Elizabeth Selma, Marcos)—inferring traits based on the people in the biographies they are reading Conference (Allessandra)—engagement strategy Conference (Desiree)—using text features
5 minutes	End of workshop share	Students work with a partner to summarize the nonfiction text they read during today's independent reading time

This is a sample conferring schedule with independent reading time divided into two chunks—one focused on whole-class goals and the other focused on individual goals.

*Look at every meeting
with students as an
opportunity for growth.
For you and for them.*

Note-Taking

Throughout the book, I've reminded you to take notes as you confer, and you may have noticed me note-taking during the conferences on video.

Here are some note-taking tips:

▸ Record the strategy you taught and the date you met with the student.

▸ Record information about strengths and possible next steps.

▸ Keep all the notes for one student on one page, whether you are meeting with them in an individual conference or a small group.

My organizational system for notes has changed over the years. For many years I used a binder with a tabbed section for each student. This allowed me to see an individual's progress over time but had its drawbacks: I couldn't share my notes with other teachers very easily, and when I met with students in groups, I had to flip between sections to write notes for each student.

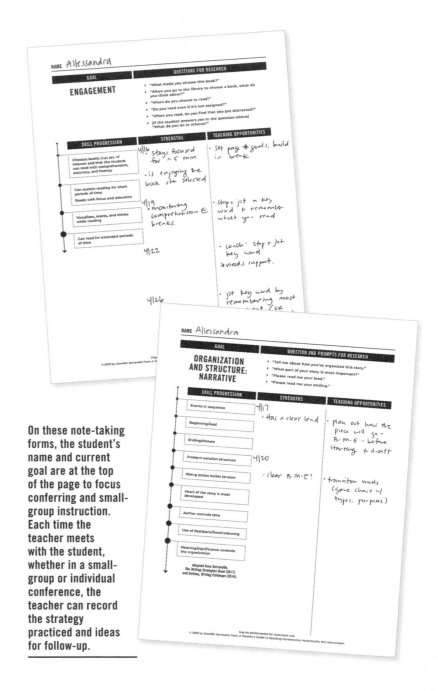

On these note-taking forms, the student's name and current goal are at the top of the page to focus conferring and small-group instruction. Each time the teacher meets with the student, whether in a small-group or individual conference, the teacher can record the strategy practiced and ideas for follow-up.

The solution I found was to move student notes out of binders and into two pocket folders—one side for reading, one for writing. I kept the folders in a basket near the classroom door and I'd grab the ones I needed for that day. Other teachers could use the notes in the folder as a way to catch up on what the student and I had worked on, and also to record notes on that same page, allowing me to see what the student had done with the other teacher. This new system worked out brilliantly, ensuring consistency of messaging between all the adults that worked with each student.

Using separate folders, I could also easily take notes during small groups: I'd open up students' individual folders in front of them and take notes in them as I made my way around to coach each student. No more flipping between tabbed sections. (Download goal-based blank note-taking forms from the online resources. 🖥)

When notes are kept in folders (rather than binders or notebooks), they are portable and can travel with the student. This is especially helpful in co-taught classrooms or for students who see additional teachers for intervention or extra support.

{ Take It to
YOUR CLASSROOM

In this chapter, I've shown you how I orchestrate the various conferring types and small groups into a sensible weekly plan. I promise you, I didn't have it this "together" when I first learned about conferring. Conferring takes practice and patience and an ability to be okay with not getting everything perfect the first time. For your own professional growth, you might decide to just spend a week or two practicing Compliment Conferences. Then a week on just Coaching Conferences. And so on. While this approach isn't exactly matching methods to purposes yet, it will allow you to develop comfort with each type of conference, which will help you be a more flexible and responsive teacher.

The most important final advice I have for you is to remember that when you meet with kids, really listen to them and try to help them. Try to keep notes in a way that works for you. Give yourself time to feel more confident with conferring, and look at every meeting with students as an opportunity for growth. For you and for them.

Works Cited

Adler, D. Cam Jansen Series. New York: Puffin Books.

Afflerbach, Peter, P. David Pearson, and Scott G. Paris. 2008. "Clarifying the Differences Between Reading Skills and Reading Strategies." *Reading Teacher* 61 (5): 364–73.

Allington, Richard L. 2008. *What Really Matters in Response to Intervention: Research-Based Designs*. New York: Pearson.

———. 2011. *What Really Matters for Struggling Readers: Designing Research-Based Programs*, 3rd ed. New York: Pearson.

Anderson, Carl. 2000. *How's It Going?* Portsmouth, NH: Heinemann.

———. 2018. *A Teacher's Guide to Writing Conferences*. Portsmouth, NH: Heinemann.

Anderson, R. C., Paul T. Wilson, and Linda G. Fielding. 1988. "Growth in Reading and How Children Spend Their Time Outside of School." *Reading Research Quarterly* 23 (3): 285–303.

Ascenzi-Moreno, Laura. 2018. "Translanguaging and Responsive Assessment Adaptations: Emergent Bilingual Readers through the Lens of Possibility." *Language Arts* 95 (6): 355–69.

Beers, Kylene. 2002. *When Kids Can't Read: What Teachers Can Do*. Portsmouth, NH: Heinemann.

Bishop, Rudine Sims. 1990. "Mirrors, Windows, and Sliding Glass Doors." *Perspectives: Choosing and Using Books for the Classroom* 6 (3): ix–xi.

Brophy, Jere E. 1981. "Teacher Praise: A Functional Analysis." *Review of Educational Research* 51 (1): 5–32.

Calkins, Lucy. 1994. *The Art of Teaching Writing*, new ed. Portsmouth, NH: Heinemann.

———. 2000. *The Art of Teaching Reading*. New York: Pearson.

———. 2017. *A Guide to the Reading Workshop*. Portsmouth, NH: Heinemann.

Calkins, Lucy, Amanda Hartman, and Zoe Ryder White. 2005. *One to One: The Art of Conferring with Young Writers*. Portsmouth, NH: Heinemann.

Calkins, Lucy, and colleagues. 2015. *Units of Study for Teaching Reading, K–5: A Grade-by-Grade Workshop Curriculum*. Portsmouth, NH: Heinemann.

Cappellini, Mary. 2005. *Balancing Reading and Language Learning*. Portland, ME: Stenhouse.

Clay, Marie M. 1993a. *An Observation Survey*. Portsmouth, NH: Heinemann.

———. 1993b. *Reading Recovery: A Guidebook for Teachers in Training*. Portsmouth, NH: Heinemann.

———. 2013. *An Observation Survey of Early Literacy Achievement*, 3rd ed. Portsmouth, NH: Heinemann.

———. 2014. *By Different Paths to Common Outcomes*. Portsmouth, NH: Heinemann.

Collins, Kathy, and Matt Glover. 2015. *I Am Reading*. Portsmouth, NH: Heinemann.

Cunningham, Patricia, and Richard L. Allington. 1999. *Classrooms That Work: They Can All Read and Write*, 2nd ed. New York: Pearson.

———. 2015. *Classrooms That Work: Where All Children Read and Write*, 6th ed. New York: Pearson.

Daane, Mary, Jay Campbell, Wendy Grigg, Madeline Goodman, and Andreas Oranje. 2005. Fourth-Grade Students Reading Aloud: NAEP 2002 Special Study of Oral Reading (NCES 2006-469). U.S. Department of Education. Institute of Education Sciences, National Center for Education Statistics. Washington, DC: Government Printing Office.

Dweck, Carol. 2006. *Mindset: The New Psychology of Success.* New York: Ballantine.

Earick, Mary. 2009. *Racially Equitable Teaching: Beyond the Whiteness of Professional Development for Early Childhood Educators.* New York: Peter Lang.

Fisher, Douglas, Nancy Frey, and John Hattie. 2017. *Teaching Literacy in the Visible Learning Classroom.* Thousand Oaks, CA: Corwin Press.

Fountas, Irene, and Gay Su Pinnell. 2016. *Fountas & Pinnell Benchmark Assessment System,* 3rd ed. Portsmouth, NH: Heinemann.

———. 2017. *The Fountas & Pinnell Literacy Continuum,* expanded ed. Portsmouth, NH: Heinemann.

Freire, Paulo. 1998. *Teachers as Cultural Workers: Letters to Those Who Dare to Teach.* Boulder, CO: Westview Press.

García, Ofelia, Jo Anne Kleifgen, and Lorraine Falchi. 2008. *From English Language Learners to Emergent Bilinguals.* A Research Initiative of the Campaign for Educational Equity. Retrieved from http://les.eric.ed.gov/fulltext/ED524002.pdf.

Gibbons, Pauline. 2015. *Scaffolding Language, Scaffolding Learning: Teaching English Learners in the Mainstream Classroom.* Portsmouth, NH: Heinemann.

Harris, Albert J., and Edward R. Sipay. 1990. *How to Increase Reading Ability: A Guide to Developmental and Remedial Methods.* London: Longman Publishing Group.

Harvey, Stephanie, and Anne Goudvis. 2007. *Strategies That Work,* 2nd ed. Portland, ME: Stenhouse.

Hattie, John. 2008. *Visible Learning.* New York: Routledge.

Hattie, John, and Shirley Clarke. 2018. *Visible Learning Feedback.* New York: Routledge.

Hattie, John, Debra Masters, and Kate Birch. 2015. *Visible Learning into Action.* New York: Routledge.

Hertz, Christine, and Kristine Mraz. 2018. *Kids First from Day One: A Teacher's Guide to Today's Classroom.* Portsmouth, NH: Heinemann.

Johnston, Peter. 2004. *Choice Words.* Portland, ME: Stenhouse.

Keene, Ellin. 2018. *Engaging Children: Igniting a Drive for Deeper Learning*. Portsmouth, NH: Heinemann.

Keene, Ellin, and Susan Zimmermann. 1997. *Mosaic of Thought*. Portsmouth, NH: Heinemann.

———. 2007. *Mosaic of Thought*, 2nd ed. Portsmouth, NH: Heinemann.

Kohn, Alfie. 1999. *Punished by Rewards: The Trouble with Gold Stars*. New York: Mariner Books.

———. 2001. "Five Reasons to Stop Saying 'Good Job!'" *Young Children*, September. www.alfiekohn.org/article/five-reasons-stop-saying-good-job/?print=pdf.

Krashen, Stephen D. 2004. *The Power of Reading: New Insights from the Research*, 2nd ed. Westport, CT: Libraries Unlimited.

Ladson-Billings, Gloria. 2009. *The Dreamkeepers: Successful Teachers of African-American Children*. San Francisco: John Wiley & Sons, Inc.

Miller, Donalyn. 2009. *The Book Whisperer: Awakening the Inner Reader in Every Child*. San Francisco: Jossey-Bass.

Miller, Debbie, and Barbara Moss. 2013. *No More Independent Reading Without Support*. Portsmouth, NH: Heinemann.

Morrell, Earnest. 2012. "Teachers as Critical Researchers: An Empowering Model for Urban Education." In *The Critical Qualitative Research Reader*, edited by Shirley Steinberg and Gaile Cannella, 364–79. New York: Peter Lang.

Moses, Lindsay. 2015. *Supporting English Learners in the Reading Workshop*. Portsmouth, NH: Heinemann.

Moss, Barbara, and Terrell A. Young. 2010. *Creating Lifelong Readers Through Independent Reading*. Newark, DE: International Reading Association.

Mulligan, Tammy, and Claire Landrigan. 2018. *It's All About the Books: How to Create Bookrooms and Classroom Libraries That Inspire Readers*. Portsmouth, NH: Heinemann.

Opitz, Michael F., and Lindsey Moses Guccione. 2009. *Comprehension and English Language Learners: 25 Oral Reading Strategies that Cross Proficiency Levels*. Portsmouth, NH: Heinemann.

Paley, Vivian. 2000. *White Teacher*, 2nd ed. Cambridge, MA: Harvard University Press.

Peterson, Ralph, and Maryann Eeds. 1990. *Grand Conversations: Literature Groups in Action*. New York: Scholastic.

Pink, Daniel. 2011. *Drive*. New York: Riverhead Books.

Pranikoff, Kara. 2017. *Teaching Talk*. Portsmouth, NH: Heinemann.

Pressley, Michael, and Richard L. Allington. 2014. *Reading Instruction That Works: The Case for Balanced Teaching*, 4th ed. New York: Guilford Press.

Ray, Katie Wood, and Matt Glover. 2011. *Watch Katie and Matt Sit Down and Teach Up*. Portsmouth, NH: Heinemann.

Richardson, Jan. 2016. *The Next Step Forward in Guided Reading*. New York: Scholastic.

Routman, Regie. 2003. *Reading Essentials: The Specifics You Need to Teach Reading Well*. Portsmouth, NH: Heinemann.

Schlechty, Phillip C. 2001. *Inventing Better Schools*. San Francisco: Jossey-Bass.

Serravallo, Jennifer. 2010. *Teaching Reading in Small Groups*. Portsmouth, NH: Heinemann.

———. 2012. *The Literacy Teacher's Playbook, Grades K–2*. Portsmouth, NH: Heinemann.

———. 2013. *The Literacy Teacher's Playbook, Grades 3–6*. Portsmouth, NH: Heinemann.

———. 2015. *The Reading Strategies Book*. Portsmouth, NH: Heinemann.

———. 2018. *Understanding Texts & Readers*. Portsmouth, NH: Heinemann.

———. 2019a. *Complete Comprehension: Fiction*. Portsmouth, NH: Heinemann.

———. 2019b. *Complete Comprehension: Nonfiction*. Portsmouth, NH: Heinemann.

Serravallo, Jennifer, and Gravity Goldberg. 2007. *Conferring with Readers: Supporting Each Student's Growth and Independence*. Portsmouth, NH: Heinemann.

Shute, Valerie J. 2007. "Focus on Formative Feedback." Educational Testing Service, March. www.ets.org/Media/Research/pdf/RR-07-11.pdf.

Souto-Manning, Mariana, and Jessica Martell. 2016. *Reading, Writing, and Talk: Inclusive Teaching Strategies for Diverse Learners, K–2*. New York: Teachers College Press.

Sulzby, Elizabeth. 1985. "Children's Emergent Reading of Favorite Storybooks: A Developmental Study." *Reading Research Quarterly* 20: 458–81.

Vygotsky, Lev S. 1978, 1934. *Mind in Society: The Development of Higher Psychological Processes*. Edited by M. Cole, V. John-Steiner, S. Scribner, and E. Souberman. Translated by A. R. Luria, M. Lopez-Morillas, and M. Cole with J. V. Wertsch. Cambridge, MA: Harvard University Press.

Wallace, C. 2013. "Bilingual Learners in a Multilingual Primary School." In *Literacy and the Bilingual Learner: Texts and Practices in London Schools*, 79–125. Basingstoke, UK: Palgrave Macmillan.

Wiggins, Grant. 2012. "Seven Keys for Effective Feedback." *Educational Leadership* 70 (1): 10–16.

———. 2013. "On So-Called 'Reading Strategies': The Utter Mess That Is the Literature and Advice to Teachers." *Granted, and . . .* (blog), March 4. https://grantwiggins.wordpress.com/2013/03/04/on-so-called-reading-strategies-the-utter-mess-that-is-the-literature-and-advice-to-teachers/.